The Value & Purpose of Management Education

Without a doubt, business schools have been a success story in higher education over the last 50 years (the period of EFMD's existence). Even so, they have come under scrutiny, and attack, over their academic legitimacy and value proposition for business and society. In this book, drawn from a special issue of *Global Focus*, the EFMD has selected around 25 of the best, most thoughtful short papers published in *Global Focus* to examine the role and purpose of EFMD in the evolution of management education.

Each of the chapters interpret current strategic debates about the evolution of business schools and their paradigms and also identify possible strategic options for handling uncertain, volatile futures. These papers can be broadly categorized into four consistent themes: the first theme is concerned with the purpose and value proposition of management education; the second theme focuses on a perceived need for new business models and how to design and build them; the third theme addresses the question of the impact of the business school on business and society given the increasingly academic pursuits of business schools and their often weak links to the business community – the so-called rigour/relevance dilemma; and the fourth theme concerns how to 'map' and design business school futures in an increasingly volatile, uncertain, complex and ambiguous crisis-oriented environment.

This impressive collection of insights from business management leaders from across the globe is inspiring reading for higher education leaders, policy makers and business leaders seeking insight into the future of management education.

Eric Cornuel is President at EFMD Global.

Howard Thomas was the inaugural Ahmass Fakahany Distinguished Professor of Global Leadership at the Questrom School, Boston University. He is also an Emeritus Professor and former Dean at Singapore Management University and a Senior Advisor at EFMD.

Matthew Wood is Director, Operations and *Global Focus* Magazine Editor at EFMD Global.

The Value & Purpose of Management Education

Looking Back and Thinking Forward in Global Focus

Edited by
Eric Cornuel, Howard Thomas and
Matthew Wood

Routledge
Taylor & Francis Group

LONDON AND NEW YORK

Cover image: Jebens Design

First published 2022
by Routledge
4 Park Square, Milton Park, Abingdon, Oxon OX14 4RN

and by Routledge
605 Third Avenue, New York, NY 10158

Routledge is an imprint of the Taylor & Francis Group, an informa business

British Library Cataloguing-in-Publication Data
A catalogue record for this book is available from the British Library

Library of Congress Cataloging-in-Publication Data
A catalog record has been requested for this book

ISBN: 978-1-032-21114-5 (hbk)
ISBN: 978-1-032-19595-7 (pbk)
ISBN: 978-1-003-26188-9 (ebk)

DOI: 10.4324/9781003261889

Designed and typeset in Din, Freight and Roboto by Jebens Design

Publisher's note
This book has been prepared from camera-ready copy provided by the authors.

Contents

The Value & Purpose of Management Education: Looking Back and Thinking Forward in Global Focus

This Open Access book is based on the 15th Anniversary Edition of Global Focus

Executive Editor
Matthew Wood / matthew.wood@efmdglobal.org

Anniversary issue edited by
Eric Cornuel
Howard Thomas
Matthew Wood

Advisory Board
Eric Cornue
Howard Thomas
John Peters

Editor-in-Chief
George Bickerstaffe

Editorial Assistant
Joanna Britton

Design & Art Direction
Jebens Design / www.jebensdesign.co.uk

Photographs & Illustrations
©Jebens Design Ltd / EFMD unless otherwise stated

Editorial & Advertising
Matthew Wood / matthew.wood@efmdglobal.org
Telephone: +32 2 629 0810

www.globalfocusmagazine.com
www.efmdglobal.org

©EFMD
Rue Gachard 88 – Box 3,
1050 Brussels, Belgium

188

210

More ways to read *Global Focus*
You can read *Global Focus* in print, online and
on the move, and in English, Chinese or Spanish

Go to globalfocusmagazine.com to
access the online library of past issues

Your say
We are always pleased to hear your thoughts on *Global Focus*,
and ideas on what you would like to see in future issues.

Please address comments and ideas to
Matthew Wood at EFMD:
matthew.wood@efmdglobal.org

"Global Focus has been an invaluable resource at the forefront of business education, highlighting the most prescient issues for the last 15 years"

Matthew Wood
Executive Editor, Global Focus

University challenge
Eric Cornuel says Europe's business schools face a testing future

Catching the tide
EU Commissioner Ján Figel welcomes EFMD involvement in education and training

Lorange sets sail
Peter Lorange is to retire as President of IMD next year. Here he talks about his long career in management education

Life at the top
Kellogg's Dean Dipak Jain on business school governance, the future of the MBA, demographics and staying on top of the rankings

Hidden dragons
How China's business schools will ultimately challenge the world

No Cambridge blues
Why Judge's Dean Among Dr Arnoud De Meyer likes being an integral part of any university

The challenge of the present

Separating the wheat from the chaff
Emerald's John Peters and Rebecca Marsh argue that academic business research needs to grow more responsibly

Into the mainstream
Koç Business School's Barış Tan is bringing management education in Turkey into the European mainstream

London calling
Sir Andrew Likierman, Dean of London Business School, on his polymath career

Should management be a profession?
Santiago Íñiguez weighs up the arguments for a semi-regulated professional association of managers

The path ahead
Ashridge's Kai Peters worries about where business schools are going

The future of management education
A high-level EFMD round table looks at the options

The man who never stopped
Andrzej Koźmiński, founder and head of Koźmiński University, one of Central and Eastern Europe's foremost business schools, on his life and achievements

Change and the future: Business education 2025
Thomas Sattelberger outlines the changing priorities and strategies that will dominate business education in 2025

Deans Across Frontiers
EFMD continues its mission to promote excellence in business and management education with a global mentoring programme

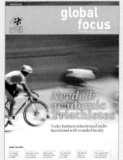

Needed: academic triathletes
Today business schools need multi-faceted and well-rounded faculty

Cox steers a new course for business schools
Sue Cox discusses her new role as EFMD vice-president

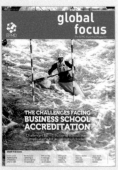

EFMD Global Focus Iss.1 Vol.11 | 2017
EFMD Global Focus Iss.3 Vol.10 | 2016
EFMD Global Focus Iss.2 Vol.10 | 2016
EFMD Global Focus Iss.1 Vol.10 | 2016
EFMD Global Focus Volume 09 | Issue 03 | 2015
EFMD Global Focus Volume 09 | Issue 02 | 2015
EFMD Global Focus Volume 09 | Issue 01 | 2015
EFMD Global Focus Volume 08 | Issue 03 | 2014
EFMD Global Focus Volume 08 | Issue 02 | 2014
EFMD Global Focus Volume 08 | Issue 01 | 2014
EFMD Global Focus Volume 07 | Issue 03 | 2013
EFMD Global Focus Volume 07 | Issue 02 | 2013
EFMD Global Focus Volume 07 | Issue 01 2013
EFMD Global Focus Volume 06 | Issue 03 2012
EFMD Global Focus Volume 06 | Issue 02 2012
EFMD Global Focus Volume 05 | Issue 03 2011
EFMD Global Focus Volume 05 | Issue 02 2011
EFMD Global Focus Volume 04 | Issue 03 2010
EFMD Global Focus Volume 04 | Issue 02 2010
EFMD Global Focus Volume 03 | Issue 03 2009
EFMD Global Focus Volume 03 | Issue 02 2009
Volume 02 | Issue 03 2008

Looking back, thinking forward

15 years of Global Focus

Without doubt, business schools have been a success story in higher education over the last 50 years (the period of EFMD's existence). Even so, they have come under scrutiny, and attack, over their academic legitimacy and value proposition for business and society

Perhaps now, in the light of the current global pandemic and continuing debates about the major associated societal challenges such as inequality, job creation, health provision and environmental sustainability, it is an opportune time to reflect on the value and purpose of management education.

We can start by examining the role and purpose of EFMD in the evolution of management education. What has been EFMD's influence as a global management education organisation in terms of its strategic developments, leadership and activities? What has it achieved over the last 50 years? What lessons were learned and not learned? What have been the persistent themes, issues and challenges over a period which included a major global financial crisis and a major pandemic? Has EFMD inspired transformative change through the diversity, identity and internationalism of Europe and European management?

There is no better place to start our reflection than with comments made in 1996 by Ray van Schaik, then EFMD President (and still a highly respected Honorary President) on the occasion of the 25th anniversary of EFMD. He outlined his vision for the role and purpose of EFMD in the management education environment, saying the organisation should:

"endeavour to continue to be a trait d'union, a link, between the corporate world and the world of education; it should continue to build and

explore a network of personal and business relationships that enable it to contribute to the process of high-quality, practical, true to life education … and finally, it should continue to cement its relationship with governments and public bodies that are involved in the process of management and education."

Indeed, it is clear that the positioning of the European business school, in particular, has been strongly influenced and shaped by the strategic role of EFMD since it was founded in 1971. EFMD has constantly focused on linking European experience and ideas in education with management practice and learning. It has emphasised internationalisation and corporate links. This outward-looking global perspective, expressed through EFMD's Euro-China Initiative, for example, led directly to the establishment of the first independent international business school in China (CEIBS – the China-European International Business School) in 1994. Following subsequent investment CEIBS is now a highly regarded world-class Asian school with significant standing and very strong international recognition in business school rankings (such as those of the *Financial Times*). Over recent years EFMD has also built a remarkable global network (EFMD-Global) counting over 750 business schools as members worldwide alongside more than 160 international associations and corporate/public sector members.

> Through Global Focus, and its other channels of knowledge generation and dissemination such as conferences, events, leadership initiatives and business school accreditations, EFMD has managed to shape, and influence the 'map' of the management education landscape globally while demonstrating its breadth and heterogenous nature

Real learning, Real impact

Jean-François Manzoni explores an international business school's experience with the EFMD Business School Impact System

As a voice for impactful management education, in 2005 EFMD started publishing *Global Focus*, a magazine with the mandate to report on the ideas, innovations, best practices of academics, managers and business schools, and disseminate them in a readable form. The magazine typically contains short articles of around 1,500 – 2,000 words, the rationale being that new knowledge should be explained clearly and in a pragmatic, applied form to stimulate readers, whether in academia, government, business or public sector organisations to implement some of these ideas in practice.

Through *Global Focus*, and its other channels of knowledge generation and dissemination such as conferences, events, leadership initiatives and business school accreditations, EFMD has managed to shape, and influence the 'map' of the management education landscape globally while demonstrating its breadth and heterogenous nature. In particular, the organisation has focused on the evolution of European management schools, clearly indicating the range of academic and business models of these schools, which have varied according to their different leadership styles and cultural and contextual influences. Generally, however, European management schools have developed a balanced and collaborative relationship with their stakeholders. The European culture and environment encourage more direct co-operation with government in order to address such issues as social inclusion, inequality, poverty and

environmental sustainability, and hence help to enhance human, social and economic progress.

Because of these contextual and cultural differences there is both a discernible 'European identity' and welcome diversity in European management models. Just as there is no common 'North American model' there is no common European model. However, a number of key themes and differentiating features clearly characterize the European management education model, including;

• The belief in socially responsible management education as proposed by organisations and communities such as the GRLI (Globally Responsible Leadership Initiative), PRME (Principles for Responsible Management Education) and the RRBM (Responsible Research in Business and Management). All of these initiatives, and others, have been carefully nurtured and supported by EFMD.
• EFMD has consistently encouraged and facilitated close collaborations between business schools and corporate organisations. This strong linkage between education and practice has stimulated investment in project-based, experiential learning and promoted growth in continuing, executive education programmes.
• Europe and the EU have embraced goals of globalisation and internationalism, and EFMD has played an important role in encouraging European schools to build an international footprint and profile. EFMD still co-sponsors

'97

Started in 1997, EFMD's EQUIS Business School accreditation process has established itself as a must have' signal of global reputation for high-quality management education

CEIBS and has had an important role in advising schools including, for example, INSEAD, EDHEC and ESSEC to locate in Singapore and elsewhere (e.g. INSEAD in Abu Dhabi).

• The Bologna Process and the European Accord in Management Education have facilitated the development of European networks and collaborations through the establishment of common degree structures and credit transfer processes. This, in turn, has encouraged the development – often with EFMD support – of pre-experience master's programmes as well as network alliances such as CEMS (the Committee of European Management Schools).

• EFMD's EQUIS Business School accreditation process (started in 1997) has established itself as a 'must have' signal of global reputation for high-quality management education. (To date, around 200 schools, across all continents, have been granted EQUIS accreditation).

• EFMD has also established similar high-quality accreditation processes for corporate learning with its 'CLIP' programme and through EOCCS which offers an evaluationof online education programmes

200

To date, around 200 schools, across all continents, have been granted EQUIS accreditation

• EFMD has also pioneered the development of network learning programmes for research directors and leadership development programmes for deans of business schools.

It can be argued, therefore, that European management educators have adopted a more balanced perspective on management education than is typically found, for example, in the more research-oriented, logical positivist perspectives of North American schools where research professors (thanks to the publish-or-perish syndrome) are viewed as the prime teaching and strategic asset.

Europeans tend to adopt the viewpoint that curricula should be balanced between teaching important formal analytic and technical skills and a range of managerial skills involving leadership and 'softer' social and psychological management skills.

Indeed, Ray van Schaik notes that softer skills, more socially responsible management, and vision and communication skills for engaging employees are critical in management education. Hence, Europeans believe strongly in a balanced philosophy of management education in which important skills of analysis, data science and digitization are nurtured, alongside a range of intellectual skills of creativity, criticism and synthesis. This balanced diet produces managers who possess a sense of social responsibility towards all stakeholders as well as a moral authority and the freedom of thought to guide and lead others well in an increasingly uncertain, complex and volatile environment.

Despite the continuing success of business and management as a field of study, there has been ongoing debate about the legitimacy, role and purpose of business schools in society particularly following the global financial crisis. However, well before that crisis the late Sumantra Ghoshal argued that business schools had been propagating and teaching amoral theories that destroyed sound managerial practices and were largely devoid of a moral and ethical compass. In essence, critical allegations of business school failure can be divided into three categories.

The first is that in terms of knowledge creation, schools research the wrong things (business school academics are allegedly not curious about what goes on inside organisations); in terms of knowledge dissemination, they teach the wrong things; and in terms of ideology, purpose and

TALKING YOUR LANGUAGE:
In addition to the English version
Global Focus is also published in
Chinese and Spanish

 For this volume we have selected around 25 of the best, most thoughtful short papers published in Global Focus. The contributions here interpret current strategic debates about the evolution of business schools and their paradigms and also identify possible strategic options for handling uncertain, volatile futures

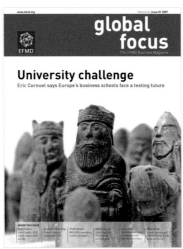

NOW AND THEN:
From the first *Global Focus* issue December 2006, to the latest from February 2021

43

In total there have been 43 issues of *Global Focus*, published across 15 volumes, plus a further 20+ Special Supplements

leadership, schools focus almost exclusively on philosophies of free market economics and are unclear about their roles in either academia or the world of practice.

Consequently, for this volume we have selected around 25 of the best, most thoughtful short papers published in *Global Focus*. The contributions here interpret current strategic debates about the evolution of business schools and their paradigms and also identify possible strategic options for handling uncertain, volatile futures. These papers can be broadly categorized into four consistent themes that recur in presentations and dialogues in conferences, books and journals and represent challenges associated with transformational change in schools for business and management. We will examine these in turn.

The first theme is concerned with the purpose and value proposition of management education; the second theme focuses on a perceived need for new business models and how to design and build them; the third theme addresses the question of the impact of the business school on business and society given the increasingly academic pursuits of business schools and their often weak links to the business community – the so-called rigour/relevance dilemma; the fourth theme concerns how to 'map' and design business school futures in an increasingly volatile, uncertain, complex and ambiguous crisis-oriented environment.

1. The Purpose and Vision of a Business School

The questions addressed by these authors focus on the overarching intent, mission and purpose of the business school, its relationship with business and the interface between schools and key stakeholders in business, government and society. Indeed, we should ask as deans, or faculty members, whether we convey a clear sense of purpose and communicate that purpose succinctly to all of our students and stakeholders. And are our activities consistent with our purpose, mission and vision?

In his paper on why Management History Matters, Professor Witzel argues on p.23 that "History teaches us to challenge the present." Why did the business models and management methods we use today evolve as they did? Why is the prevailing orthodoxy what it is? What other competing models and methods emerged and why were they discarded? Are we really managing in the best possible way we can? He concedes that "history does not have all the answers but it does have some of them." And, quoting Professor John Maynard Keynes, who wrote during the 1929-39 Great Depression, he states that "we must study the present in light of the past for the purposes of the future." In essence, while history hardly ever repeats itself it does help to unravel those forces and influences which shape events so avoiding the mistakes of "military generals who try to fight the next war using the methods of the last one."

From the perspective of a former editor of the *Financial Times*, Sir Richard Lambert, business wants, from business schools, "great graduates and relevant ideas." He suggests that in an uncertain and challenging world undergoing profound transformation, business schools will need leaders who possess, at least, four key qualities and skills: managing and embracing diversity; dealing with uncertainty; understanding of the role and machinery of government; and understanding the role, responsibilities and purpose of business itself. In his view, business leaders need guidance from business schools about new ideas and fresh thinking about their roles and responsibilities.

Interestingly, Della Bradshaw, the highly regarded management editor at the *Financial Times* (FT) for over two decades (starting in 1995), points out that Richard Lambert, then editor at the FT, "was keen on the idea of (business school rankings) and that it

In an uncertain and challenging world undergoing profound transformation, business schools will need leaders who possess, at least, four key qualities and skills: managing and embracing diversity; dealing with uncertainty; understanding of the role and machinery of government; and understanding the role, responsibilities and purpose of business itself

was something the newspaper believed it could do well." She explained that "the idea behind the ranking ... was – and still is – to produce a listing of business schools around the world that are educating global managers for the 21st century." In order to do this well she noted "the FT ranking measures three main criteria: the career progression of graduates; the international focus of the programme; and the research capabilities of a business school." While the research criterion attracted controversy, it was seen as a measure of 'thought leadership' and innovation as "we (at the FT) wanted to find out where the new ideas were coming from." Simply put, "the FT ranking was initially driven by the newspaper feeling that this was something it could do well and European schools wanting something to put them on a global stage" since schools such as INSEAD, IMD and LBS, believed that North American rankings such as 'Business Week' (launched in 1987) concentrated almost exclusively on U.S. schools and did not give them enough exposure.

Eric Cornuel, the President of EFMD has stressed that "Della has absolutely no equal in the press world in terms of knowledge and understanding of management education." Indeed, she has been both a strong supporter of, and a catalyst for change, in management education. She indicates that change in the last two decades has shown "the relative decline of the U.S. education market as it has faced

real challenges form the growing numbers and quality of business schools and programmes in regions such as Europe and Africa. Added to this has been the growing diversity of academic programmes offered by schools particularly in the categories of specialized Masters programmes and pre-experience Masters programmes (an area strongly influenced by European business schools).

Ray van Schaik, Honorary President of EFMD, also draws on his many years of experience as a European Chairman and CEO (Heineken), in the light of the global economic crisis, about the social responsibility of a business school in preparing students for societal change. He argues that business schools did not cause the economic crisis, but they have a key role to play in determining what comes next. In particular, he focuses (p.18) on the need to demonstrate to students "that by managing a company in a socially responsible way you can still maximise profits, and can still contribute to the welfare of interested parties but also to society at large thus winning the trust and acceptance of the general public and securing the continuity of your business." He notes that as business schools rethink their curricula they should focus much more on 'soft skills' and creative thinking than enhancing management techniques, "after all, techniques are a help but ultimately you manage with your guts — now more then ever." Schools also need to be more outward-looking than ever before, which will bring them into close working contact with their market (business or government) and make sure that their views are heard in society."

Former President and university professor, Arnoud de Meyer of SMU, argues that "business schools need to become 'Schools for business'" (p.28). In his words "This is a paradigm shift for the world's business schools, a tipping point if scholars and researchers break out of their comfort zones." He notes that both disciplinary and inter-disciplinary research are important and critical for schools of business to be of value to business and society in the following terms: "The business world exists as an ecosystem of business, government, NGOs and non-profits, each interlocking with the other. This is also why research has to be interdisciplinary, to consider the impact across different stakeholders." He provides a range of examples drawn from his presidential tenure at SMU and demonstrates (p.29) how it "has anchored a distinctive brand of

holistic, "broad-based education" to develop collaborative (not command and control) graduates and leaders who will make a difference to society."

Howard Thomas and Ken Starkey examine the viewpoint of five expert scholars: Martin Kitchener, Rick Delbridge (Cardiff Business School); Colin Mayer (Said Business School, Oxford), Armand Hatchuel (Ecole des Mines, Paris) and Alan Irwin (Copenhagen Business School) about the value and purpose of business and management education. Kitchener and Delbridge examined the notion of a public value business school, whose purpose is directed towards social and economic development; Meyer stressed that business should be a force for the greater good by contributing to a wide range of social and economic stakeholders rather than simply maximising shareholder value; Hatchuel in a similar vein sought how to redefine the meaning of a business enterprise while Irwin argued that impactful research in business schools should focus on both narrow disciplinary issues as well as interdisciplinary research addressing the ground challenges of society such as limits to growth. The outcome of these papers was a consensus that "business schools should be far more proactive in addressing the many challenges we face in these troubling times."

Overall, from these six papers a clear view emerges that business schools are too complacent. The mission of the business school is often seen as too narrow and focused. It does not espouse a distinct philosophy and is not anchored well in terms of its broad societal influence. It often lacks a coherent agenda and the lessons of history have not always been learned. But business schools have become increasingly aware of the need to change. And, as the writers of these papers indicate, schools have the scholarly and theoretical ability to be creative, proactive and shape agendas either by themselves or in consortia or through their societies. However, it is only recently that they have seized the initiative or understood how to work well with their business ecosystems.

2. Business Models, and the Paradigm Trap

There is a clear view that management as a field many have become stuck in a paradigm trap surrounded by a set of inherent dogmas and dominant logics. In particular, critics point to the dominant logic of the Anglo-North American design,

reflecting an obsolete model, with outdated course materials, textbooks and case studies, as the main culprit.

It is argued that business schools have mimicked this dominant logic in order to be seen as serious players and strong competitors for the top elite schools (historically often from North America). Where there have been innovations generally the new models have been incremental (either practice or discipline-oriented) rather than radical, and have rarely involved comprehensive re-thinking of existing paradigms to reflect future growth paths of new, often technologically-based, industries and new forms of competition, public and private.

Recent extensive research interest in business models has increased understanding of business model innovation, yet few business school scholars or deans, have looked in the mirror to evaluate, or refresh, the business model of their business schools.

The first two papers from Cornuel and Shenton/ Houdayer discuss the further development of a European model and approach in management education. Eric Cornuel, the President of EFMD, in his article 'University Challenge' believes that European models of management education are differentiated and distinctive because of their broader stakeholder

'97

The quality and reputation of European schools globally has also increased substantially through the wide acceptance of EFMD's EQUIS accreditation process, launched in 1997

One of the problems of management education remains its continuing (although reduced) emphasis on the teaching of functional disciplines when, in reality, managers work in a cross-disciplinary, even multi-disciplinary world. So many different elements interact with each other that managers must be capable of a broader view

focus, people orientation and strong emphasis on cultural and humanistic values. However, historically they suffer from resource constraints and shortages. He argues that the greatest obstacle to change is "that most European universities are largely state-funded rather than having diversified funding sources." Nevertheless, he notes that the challenge of the pervasive globalization of management education has created opportunities to enhance the quality and reputation of European management education approaches.

Both Cornuel and Shenton/Houdayer in their article on the 'Bologna effect' believe that the Bologna Accord and higher education process has significantly improved the value and effectiveness of European models by harmonizing academic degree standards, credit transfer and quality assurance standards by creating a European Higher Education Arena. In this arena a significant effect has been the development of a European Masters Market in which 'readable' degree titles, whether for specialized, pre-experience or post-experience general management degrees, have proven to be significant marketing advantages both in European and global markets thus increasing the competitiveness and resourcing of European schools. The quality and reputation of European schools globally has also increased substantially through the wide acceptance of EFMD's EQUIS accreditation process (launched in 1997) but also the strong positioning of a wider range of European schools in the prestigious *Financial Times* rankings category for pre-experience master's programmes in which European schools have led the way. As Shenton and Houdayer note "Thanks to the convergent impact of Bologna, of accreditation and of the rankings, European business schools and university faculties of business are potentially in a much stronger competitive position internationally."

Cornuel's plea for the importance of curriculum and model change can be captured in a précis of some of the key statements in his article as follows: "One of the problems of management education remains its continuing (although reduced) emphasis on the teaching of functional disciplines when, in reality, managers work in a cross-disciplinary, even multi-disciplinary world. So many different elements interact with each other that managers must be capable of a broader view."

Further, in addressing required capabilities and competencies he states, "developing the

www.globalfocusmagazine.com

competencies, capacities and attitudes requires more than relying solely on the simple acquisition of knowledge. Experiential, propositional and practical ways of learning must be integrated into the curriculum."

He also stresses very strongly the role of leadership: "We need to focus on leadership because too often today we encounter a management style that is somewhat harsh, that confronts people rather than supports them, that punishes them for mistakes and that focusses only on shareholder value. As a result, people are stressed and ill at ease in their work. I believe that we must encourage more human (and humane) values in management, especially forgiveness and health at work."

Kai Peters and Howard Thomas broaden the debate on business models in their paper on 'A Sustainable Model for Business Schools' when they question the sustainability of current financial models echoing the substance of Cornuel's arguments about the European resourcing challenge. Indeed, they argue that the current business model of business schools is "financially unstable and probably unsustainable." They note that an escalation in the tuition fees of MBA and EMBA programmes, the traditional business school 'cash cows', cannot be sustained as the students' return on investment is often called into question (except for perhaps the elite schools). Further revenue from other sources e.g. donations, executive education – generally are not reliable and therefore, do not solve the resourcing problem. Consequently, they add that many institutions area using a very "luxurious" faculty model where faculty costs, perhaps for demand/ supply reasons, are a very high percentage of a school's expenditure. Yet the highest paid faculty often teach far less than more education-oriented faculty. They question "how long can this go on?" They note that this unsustainability issue is likely to be much more challenging in university-based business schools.

Peters, Smith and Thomas in a comprehensive review of 'The Business of Business Schools' amplify the theme of the financial challenges facing the modern, business school outlined in their sustainability paper. They note that the advent of the rankings era in the late 1980s changed the higher aims and focus of business school deans from consistently improving the quality of their educational offerings to one where strategies of competitive

positioning, involving PR, marketing, branding, etc., are an increasing part of the 'business of business schools'. This hyper-competitive era came to rule their world. Using value chain-models they show for example, how the value of 'high priced' EMBA programmes can be compared with often price-regulated undergraduate programmes from a financial perspective. Hence, they question how some business schools can compete and survive in this hyper-competitive arena.

Santiago Iniguez in 'Needed: Academic Triathletes' takes up the theme of strengthening the links between academia and the business school market in order to highlight the need to hire a breed of excellent, multi-talented faculty (often called 'ambidextrous professors') in the modern business-oriented, business school environment. These 'academic triathletes', multi-faceted and well-rounded, are essential in a business school model in which faculty must demonstrate excellence in research, teaching and interaction/involvement with business and government.

Edeltraud Hanappi-Eggers paper 'Assessing Academics' Performance' examines how business schools should assess faculty across all of the attributes of the 'triathlete' model. Her laudable aim is to develop a performance evaluation-model that goes "beyond research/publication and fairly weighs teaching excellence, knowledge dissemination to business and industry, industry, and service and contribution to the school's reputation for high-quality excellence in management education."

3. Rigour-Relevance and Business School Impact

There is a clear rift between management education and management practice. In many business schools this is exacerbated by business school faculty, and their deans, stressing a research-driven model of rigorous, academic research in management rather than a more balanced model of theoretical and more practical applied research.

Consequently, many business schools have been criticized for trailing behind in impacting or influencing management practice. A leadership dilemma for deans is how to bridge Andrew Pettigrew's so-called rigour-relevance gap and to lead the field in shaping and changing management practices. Hence, it is argued that management educators should increasingly focus attention to

Among respondents to the *Tomorrow's MBA* survey the full-time MBA is still the preference of 48% of prospective students though 34% prefer part-time study and 18% choose distance learning. Blended learning is also the most popular approach to studying for 27% while just 18% choose traditional academic terms and office hours.

The Graduate Management Admissions Council (GMAC), guardian of the GMAT, has also reported that just over two-thirds (67%) of two-year full-time MBA programmes experienced a decline in application volume in 2011 compared with 2010, continuing a trend that began in 2009.

Over five years, those taking the GMAT aged under 24 grew from 58,688 in 2006-07 to 91,028 in 2010-11. Among the 24-30 age group numbers have also grown over the same period (from 114,961 to 124,878) but are down from a peak of 130 2008-09. The number of test take old has also declined duri The data sugg learnin

48%

The survey reveale that the full-time M is still the preferenc of 48% of prospectiv students though 34% prefer part-time study and 18% choose distance learning

91k

Over five years, those taking the GMAT aged under 24 grew from 58,688 in 2006-07 to 91,028 in 2010-11, the 24-30 age group numbers have grown over the same period (from 114,961 to 124,878) b

50

In essence, BSIS is an impact auditing and measurement approach which has been applied to around 50 different schools around the globe

assessing the relevance and impact of their research not only in terms of academic research (knowledge generation) but also the impact implications of that research for management practice and society more broadly as a whole, in terms of economic and social development and associated policy initiatives.

In other words, balanced excellence means that business school academics must aspire to deliver outputs that meet the double-hurdle of scholarly quality and policy/practice impact. That is an ongoing challenge which is closely related to the need for business schools to evaluate the impact of their knowledge generation (research) activities as well as the direct impact of those intellectual contributions to management practice.

The relevance gap in business schools addresses the balance between scholarly academic research and its consequent impact on practice. It is often termed the 'rigour-relevance' problem or an Andrew Pettigrew frames it in his article 'Scholarly Impact and the Co-Production Hypothesis' the 'double-hurdle' problem – namely "scholars in the area should have the aspiration to do scholarly and practical work to tackle the 'double hurdle'" (p.8). He goes on to say that "It's rare to find people who aspire to produce work at the highest scholarly quality and deal with practical issues at the same time." His solution to making management research more relevant to practitioners is to co-produce significant

and meaningful business school research. "Co-production means the involvement of (business) partners with academics throughout the complete cycle of research ... the hypothesis here is that early and continuous (business) engagement should increase the probability of engagement" (p.11). In essence, co-production of impactful knowledge in business schools should mirror the positive experience of such activity in many engineering schools.

Michael Kalika and Gordon Shenton in their article 'Impact: Is It Enough Just to Talk About It?' address the challenge of how to measure it. They examine what impact means and outline the multiple forms of impact (e.g. financial, educational, business development, intellectual, regional ecosystem, regional image, societal, etc.) in order to assess the nature and extent of the impact a business school has on its immediate environment. They explain the logic behind BSIS (the Business School Impact Survey) pioneered by FNEGE in France and adopted as a service for EFMD members. In essence, BSIS is an impact auditing and measurement approach which has been applied to around 50 different schools around the globe.

A number of papers which follow the BSIS paper illustrate the impact of BSIS measurement on three different but well-regarded management schools, namely IMD, St Gallen and the Sobey School.

One of the clear lessons from the past is the need to change, adjust and adapt the 'business model' of business schools in relation to mission, purpose, governance, knowledge development and meaningful impact. Thus, approaches involving scenarios, open innovation and foresight models will become increasingly common

Jean-François Manzoni, President of IMD, Switzerland outlines the school's experiences in the paper entitled Real Learning, Real Impact. It is clear that the school found the process to be of great value, and released the 44-page report on impact findings as a public report. In fact, Manzoni notes that (during a recent meeting) "the Mayor of Lausanne expressed his pleasant surprise at the size of IMD's local financial impact. He had simply no idea it was that high. Since then we (at IMD) have continued to take the language and the local connection lesson to heart and we have been communicating more of our research, thought-leadership and campus news in French." Similarly, Thomas Bieger, President at St Gallen, in his article 'How Being Embedded in Your Region Helps Growth' explains how through using BSIS the School learned how to further consolidate and build on its local roots. This theme is echoed by Patricia Bradshaw and Erin Elaine Casey of the Sobey School in Nova Scotia, Canada. The collective impact of their School on the local community of Halifax and the province of Nova Scotia was recognized strongly by the provincial legislature. It is a story of how a small business school in an important gateway for Canada created significant, meaningful impact for the Nova Scotia ecosystem. It led to an enhanced sense of pride, identity and purpose for the School and the wider business and government community in the region.

The theme of 'growing the impact of management education and scholarship' was also discussed in our article, jointly written by the President/Rectors of specialist 'universities for business and management' including Université Paris Dauphine, University of St. Gallen (HSG), Singapore Management University (SMU), University of Copenhagen Business School (CBS) and FGV-EBAPE (the Brazilian School of Public and Business Administration). These universities "without exception embrace inter-multi-and transdisciplinary curricula ... and tend to have strong engagement with practitioners, public agencies; and inform professionals, practitioners and policy-makers of the latest research findings." They quote Howard Thomas and Michelle Lee from SMU who "have advocated a holistic student perspective on management (not a silo-oriented one) that will encourage the development of integrative thinkers who, in management careers, will be more likely to make decisions "with integrity, reflection and a moral and ethical compass." They offer, beyond gaining society's trust, four clear contributions for the future development of impactful management education including "interdisciplinary mindsets, global mindsets, stakeholder engagement, sustainability and innovation with tradition."

Two further contributions to impactful research are provided by Anne Tsui, a former President of

44

It is clear that IMD found the BSIS process to be of great value, and released 'Real Learning, Real Impact' a 44-page report on impact findings as a public report

the Academy of Management in the U.S. and Paul Beaulieu, a Canadian academic. They both argue for socially responsible scholarship and more comprehensive and responsible social engagement.

Anne Tsui's (the founder of RRBM, the Responsible Research for Business and Management Community) paper 'Reconnecting with the Business World' proposes that it is time for all parties in the business enterprise – scholars, school leaders, grant agencies, policy makers, business leaders and journal editors – to contribute to the pursuit of socially responsible leadership by remembering "the goal of science; the discovery and application of true knowledge to improve the human condition." Professor Beaulieu in his paper 'Intentional Impact from Business Schools' suggests, in a similar manner to Professor Tsui that "there is now an emerging consensus on the agenda's priority. Business schools of all organizational configurations must care proactively for the future of humanity and for the societies they exist to serve."

4. Uncertain Futures and Transformational Change

It is absolutely clear from critical writings and commentaries over the last two decades that management education is at a crossroads (a 'tipping point'). The path forward is complicated not only by rapid changes in technology and global trade but also the impacts of a very severe and extensive global pandemic on economic development. One of the clear lessons from the past is the need to change, adjust and adapt the 'business model' of business schools in relation to mission, purpose, governance, knowledge development and meaningful impact. Thus, approaches involving scenarios, open innovation and foresight models will become increasingly common.

Business schools have generally not innovated in a consistent fashion and have been complacent. They have been stuck in similar models, or paradigms for several decades that have changed only incrementally over time. Their impacts on business, government and society have been equally insignificant and there is a need for stronger partnerships and tri-sector collaborations (with government, business and society) as they search for greater societal legitimacy and impact.

Charles Handy in his article 'The Past is not the Future' uses the metaphor of a 'second curve' as a framework from which business schools and their stakeholders can glimpse into the future and find a 'second curve' which will enable them to survive and prosper. Handy's sense from drawing on the EFMD publications by Howard Thomas, and others, on the Future of Management Education is that most business schools are at, or even beyond, the first curve of their development and at a 'tipping point'. Just as the businesses they serve are becoming ever more complex and large and facing questions about their legitimacy, so are the business schools. Hence Handy argues that "the opportunity is there for business schools to match their second curves to those of the corporations." He suggests that the teaching/education aspects should be covered by online courses and that management education should concentrate on manager development – "it means moving away from the university and towards the work organisation" – becoming 'think tanks' exploring the future of business, of capitalism, of organisation structures and the role of regulation and so on."

Christos Pitelis, in his article 'A Future for Business Education' argues that "the evolution of business education has gone from practice to theory and back to practice. I think, however, that the reality is more nuanced than that. What we see is a re-emergent focus on teaching, engagement, relevance and impact, taking place from stronger conceptual foundations – that of 'engaged scholarship' – that could be imparted to, and co-developed with the student body and other stakeholders" (through collaborative and meaningful 'partnerships'). This argument mirrors very closely Pettigrew's views on scholarship with impact; and amplifies those with similar pleas about the need for interdisciplinarity and developing, through engaged scholarship, the field's own concepts, theories and methods rather than on over reliance on disciplines such as economics. The key message of Pitelis and from a recent EFMD seminar on the future of business schools (held at Nottingham Business School and chaired by Professor Ken Starkey) was the "need to think – who we are and what we might become in the light of a history that possessed a number of alternative paths" … "We also need to recognize what we have lost in terms of a particular path that is embedded (some might say 'embalmed') in league and ranking tables such as those of the *Financial Times* and B*usiness Week*." It was noted, however, that there has been much to praise and much promise in what we have achieved — "Our challenge is that much of the promise has not yet been fully realized and we may be losing legitimacy as a result."

Santiago Iniguez, one of the pioneers in online learning at IE Business School in Spain, explains why 'the future is blended' arguing that conventional face-to-face teaching can be augmented and enhanced by using technology, such as online learning, in the management education process. For Iniguez, whose blended learning programmes at Instituto de Empresa, Madrid are seen as innovative and progressive, "the key instructional and pedagogical question" is not whether blended learning is the future or whether classroom teaching is more effective than online teaching but rather, "what is the optimal blend of online and face-to-face learning?"

Howard Thomas's paper 'Apply Liberally' contains a strong argument that management education should be anchored in a tradition of liberal education in which the more analytic, technological and specialized of management aspects are balanced by a sound grounding, and understanding of the wider world through study of the humanities and the social sciences. Thomas gives a concrete example of what liberal management education means in practice through discussing his experiences in developing and adapting SMU's liberal, holistic and broadly-based, multi-disciplinary undergraduate programme (p.23). Arnoud de Meyer's paper on 'The DNA of Business Schools: Schools for Business', in the section on the purpose/mission of business schools, also explains the broad philosophy of liberal education in SMU, but adds the proposition that SMU's liberal education philosophy extends to the overall strategic intent of SMU as a university with a mission to serve, through its teaching/research and service programmes, society as a whole.

Jordi Canals, a former Dean at IESE in Barcelona, Spain asks in his paper 'Can They Fix It' whether business schools will be able to deal with the challenges of the future, and attend to deficits amplified by the global financial crisis, if they want to remain relevant. He focuses particularly on aspects of the schools mission and purpose identifying deficits in mission, governance and humanistic orientations noting that: "As institutions, education managers and business leaders, business schools have to rethink the role of companies in

"The world is more prosperous than ever before and yet our societies are marked by uncertainty and unease." Business schools cannot ignore this shadow of uneasiness personified by five elements, namely the rise of the precariat (those at the bottom of society's pyramid), anti-globalization, anti-intellectualism, extreme inequality and tolerance of greater asymmetry

society and the job of business leaders." He argues from a stakeholder perspective that "there is a need to make firms more human, moving beyond the notion of pure efficiency." It is clear that he believes schools must get closer to businesses and through joint projects and partnerships improve the relevance of their research for management practice and, hence learn how to promote life-long learning between schools and their stakeholders.

Johan Roos, formerly Dean at Jönköping and now Chief Academic Officer at Hult International Business School, in his paper 'Casting Light in the Shadows' is in agreement with Canals, that despite growing success, business schools need to find a grander vision of purpose, and community, to counter emerging shadows. He quotes President Obama to support this need for a grander vision as follows: "The world is more prosperous than ever before and yet our societies are marked by uncertainty and unease." He argues that business schools cannot ignore the shadow of uneasiness personified by five elements, namely the rise of the precariat (those at the bottom of society's pyramid), anti-globalization, anti-intellectualism, extreme inequality and tolerance of greater asymmetry. Roos believes that we must prevent this shadow overtaking us in business schools and, therefore, move towards a grander

vision for the role that business schools play in creating our collective future. "Business schools should become the light bearers of hope, change and global community." His vision encompasses a range of objectives, from creating relevant, innovative and practical solutions for the benefit of the broader society to being enablers of global prosperity that open doorways to help the precariat achieve social and financial inclusion.

This theme of a grander vision links well with Anne Tsui's paper in Section 3 in which she explains the aims of RRBM to inspiring, encouraging and supporting research that is both credible and contributes to socially responsible research and leadership about the grand challenges of society. For example, research about inclusive growth includes examining the need for financial and social inclusion for the precariat, means extending basic rights for all to access and participate in the vital networks of services and know-how that are the indispensable enablers of increasing productivity in society (Thomas, H. and Hedrick-Wong, Y. RRBM/IACMR Award Seminar, 11th December 2020).

 Audio version

Section_01
The Purpose and Vision of a Business School

"Writing during the Great
Depression, the economist
John Maynard Keynes wrote
that 'we must study the present
in light of the past for the purposes
of the future'. Those words
have never been more true"

Morgan Witzel
'Into the mainstream'

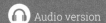 Audio version

Volume   Issue

03_03

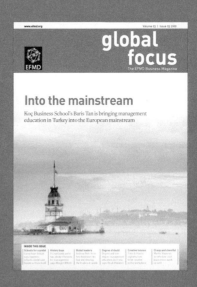

2009

The economic crisis has prompted many to call for a greater emphasis on studying the history of business and management. **Morgen Witzel** looks at the lessons that could be learned and why they are so important

Why management history matters...

We are often told that management, as both a set of practices and a body of theory, has only emerged within the last 100 years or so. The first books on operations management were published in the 1890s; the first texts on marketing and "labour management" (as HRM used to be called) appeared in the following decade. Business strategy did not emerge until the 1960s and it was not until the 1980s that anyone began writing or talking about knowledge management.

Because of this and because the pace of change in the world today is such that management theories and practices are having to be constantly re-invented, it might be assumed that there is not much point in studying the history of management. But that assumption would be wrong.

In fact, although the first coherent bodies of management theory are indeed only about a century old, many of the management practices we use today go back thousands of years. And although the pace of change is certainly very rapid, some things in management – the need to motivate employees, the need to create value for customers, the need to manage risk – have not changed at all.

> *Although the first coherent bodies of management theory are indeed only about a century old, many of the management practices we use today go back thousands of years*

Consider the following:

– The first text to set out the responsibilities of a manager, *The Duties of the Vizier*, was written in ancient Egypt more than 3,500 years ago

– The first brands – identifying marks on products that gave the customer an assurance of quality and established the maker's reputation – appeared in China in the 11th century

– One of the richest men in Renaissance Italy, Giovanni d'Amerigo Benci, was a professional salaried manager who worked his way up from the position of accounts clerk to become managing partner of the Medici Bank, Europe's biggest business of its day.

The first modern business school, set up for the purpose of teaching managers to do their jobs efficiently and effectively, was established by the East India Company in 1805, 104 years before the founding of Harvard Business School.

When we look at any of the great monuments of the past – the Egyptian pyramids, the Great Wall of China, the Roman network of roads and towns, the cathedrals of the Middle Ages – we at once find evidence of managers, people whose role was to motivate and guide the efforts of others so as to get things done.

3500

The first text to set out the responsibilities of a manager, *The Duties of the Vizier*, was written in ancient Egypt more than 3,500 years ago

130,000

The 14th century Italian merchant, Francesco Datini, spent half his working life gathering knowledge of markets and trading conditions. The 130,000 letters he accumulated during his lifetime represent one of the great business archives of all time

Nor were their managerial methods entirely *ad hoc*. There are plenty of texts on management in many fields – business, civil administration, the military – ranging from ancient Rome to the Middle Ages.

In the early 15th century the Italian theologian Bernardino of Siena set out his own views on managerial competencies. Good managers, he said, had to be efficient; they had to be hard working; they should be willing to assume responsibility; and they should not be afraid to take risks. Five hundred years on, his words are still true.

Fads and fancies in organisations come and go but the basic principles of what an organisation is and what it should do were understood by St Benedict of Nursia in the 6th century when he wrote the rule of the Benedictine Order of monks.

As well as describing the monks' religious duties, the rule also laid down procedures for reporting and control, stated the overall purpose of the organisation, defined its function and mission, and defined the role of each member of the organisation in helping to achieve its purpose. Similar rules were adopted by other religious orders, hospitals, universities, governments, guilds and businesses, and the same basic model is still in use today.

One of the fundamental concepts of marketing – that it is the consumer not the producer who defines value – was set out by the theologian St Thomas Aquinas in the 13th century. Branding, as we have seen, was invented even earlier. Proto-marketers also knew how to use psychological cues to evoke a response in potential consumers long the before the first theories of marketing – or, for that matter, of psychology – were set out.

The importance of information and knowledge was understood by the Italian merchant Francesco Datini in the late 14th century. Datini estimated he spent

" "

One of the fundamental concepts of marketing – that it is the consumer not the producer who defines value – was set out by the theologian St Thomas Aquinas in the 13th century

half his working life corresponding with other people and gathering knowledge of markets and trading conditions. He carefully archived his letters so that he could go back to them if needed (the 130,000 letters he accumulated during his lifetime represent one of the great business archives of all time).

And hundreds of years before the first books and articles on strategy appeared we can find managers in companies large and small assessing strategic options, scanning the environment and making and implementing strategic plans. Generic strategies such as product and market diversification were known, and used, for centuries before the age of Igor Ansoff and Michael Porter.

The early academic writers on management closer to our own time knew this. Paul Cherington, first professor of marketing at Harvard Business School, commented that the purpose of his research was to document and record best practice so that it could be taught to others; he made no claim to having invented marketing.

Lyndall Urwick, regarded by some as the founder of management consultancy in Britain, wrote in 1933 that the origins of modern marketing could be traced back at least to the 17th century and probably further.

What does this mean for the modern manager?

There are at least three reasons why knowledge of management in the past is vitally important and has the potential to help managers today and tomorrow to do their jobs more effectively.

First, an understanding of how management was done in the past can help to prevent managers – and consultants and theorists – from reinventing the wheel. This is something to which modern management is very much prone. In their recent book on management innovations, *Giant Steps in Management*, Michael Mol and Julian Birkinshaw comment that "rather like the propensity of Hollywood directors for remaking classic movies in contemporary settings, management thinkers are very good at reconceptualizing old ideas, giving them a new twist and packaging them for an audience that wasn't exposed to the original idea".

For example, business process re-engineering (BPR), one of the great management fads of the 1990s, was in effect little more than Taylorism (the theory of scientific management developed by Frederick Taylor in the late 19th century) repackaged – "scientific management for the information age" in the words of one critic.

> *History does not have all the answers. But it does have some of them and in uncertain times, anything that can help businesses to survive and prosper should be welcomed*

And thanks to their lack of experience and knowledge, the re-inventers often end up by building square wheels or ones that will not fit on the axle.

In the late 1990s, many Internet retailers, operating in what they saw as a totally new business environment, discarded the rule books on marketing, convinced that none of the old logic applied. Many, like the now infamous clothing retailer Boo.com, found out too late that this was not so.

They had wonderful websites that attracted customers but they were unable to fulfil orders. The result was widespread customer dissatisfaction. Had they taken the precaution of looking at a very similar business model developed 100 years earlier by catalogue retailers such as Montgomery Ward and Sears they would have seen the importance of fulfilment and understood the vital role played by distribution.

Second, studying how management methods and practices have changed (or remain unchanged) helps us to understand the role of change in management. Of central importance is the realisation that every new management method or technique evolves in response to a set of drivers.

Some of these come from within organisations: the need for greater efficiency, the need to retain the best employees, the need to use knowledge more effectively and become more innovative, and so on. Others come from external pressures: customer demand, macro-economic forces, changing social priorities, the emergence of new technologies and the like.

History teaches us that each set of circumstances generates a managerial response. The very high levels of risk run by businesses in the Middle Ages led to a series of strategic and organisational responses. Many businesses used limited-life partnerships to draw in key strategic partners for short periods of time, remaining flexible so that they could move swiftly to adapt to changing circumstances. They also diversified, across both product ranges and geographies, in order to lay off risks.

In the 18th century at the start of the Industrial Revolution firms developed pyramidal hierarchies of management in order to meet the challenges of controlling large centralised organisations. Conversely, in the 19th century the entrepreneur Julius Reuter invented a kind of prototype of the virtual organisation when setting up his international news wire service.

When we look beyond the techniques and practices of the managers themselves to the drivers that created those practices, we can gain valuable insights into our own time. What drivers exist today and what managerial responses are being created? How do we as managers respond to pressures by innovating and developing new practices? What determines whether these practices are the right ones and will work?

That leads in turn to the third reason why management history matters. Many of us assume that the management methods we use today are the best available. They have been studied, tested, analysed by the best academic brains and taught at the best business schools. Therefore, they must represent what the scientific management pioneer Frank Gilbreth once called the "One Best Way" of managing.

But history teaches us that what is right for one place and time, for one company in one set of circumstances will not always work for others. Management methods do need to change with the times. Those that try to manage using the methods and business models of the past are like generals who prepare to fight the next war using the methods that won the last one.

History teaches us to challenge the present. Why did the business models and management methods we use today evolve as they did? Why is the prevailing orthodoxy what it is? What other competing models and methods emerged and why were they discarded? Are we really managing in the best possible way that we can?

It is far too much to claim that the current financial crisis might have been avoided if managers had studied more history (although by encouraging bankers and others to challenge the prevailing orthodoxy it might have helped prevent some mistakes or mitigated their effects).

History does not have all the answers. But it does have some of them and in uncertain times anything that can help businesses to survive and prosper should be welcomed.

Writing during the Great Depression, the economist John Maynard Keynes wrote that "we must study the present in light of the past for the purposes of the future". Those words have never been more true. **gf**

ABOUT THE AUTHOR

Morgen Witzel is honorary senior fellow at the University of Exeter Business School in the UK and a senior consultant with the Winthrop Group of business historians. His book *Management History: Text and Cases* will be published in November 2009 by Routledge.

Section_01
The Purpose and Vision of a Business School

"Successful leaders of the future will need judgment, imagination and the capacity to work in unfamiliar surroundings if they are to make the most of these extraordinary shifts in global power balances"

Sir Richard Lambert
'What does business want from business schools?'

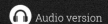 Audio version

Volume

Issue

06_03

gf

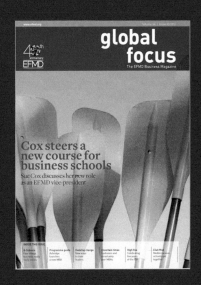

2012

What does business want from business schools?

What does business want from business schools? The answer is: "exactly what it has always wanted" – great graduates and relevant ideas.

But the qualities required of those graduates and the nature of the ideas that are of most interest to business are both changing radically. The world is undergoing a profound transformation in economic, political and social terms – on a scale and at a pace never seen before. As a result, tomorrow's business leaders are going to need a new set of skills to handle these challenges.

And the question that readers of *Global Focus* have to answer is: are business schools as they are currently structured, teaching programmes as they are currently designed best equipped to deliver them?

Of course, there is no single answer to the question. But my guess is that quite a lot of schools still have much to do to keep up with the game in this fast-changing world. This article concentrates on just four of the qualities that businesses will require of their future leaders in this time of transformation. (There are, of course, many more.)

Sir Richard Lambert suggests four key issues

" " " *Our understanding of globalisation is
becoming much more subtle and nuanced
than was the case in an America-centric world*

Embracing diversity

The first, and in some ways the most important, is the ability to manage diversity. Consider this. During the 1990s, just 12 countries in the world generated growth in incomes per head at a pace that was twice the OECD average. In the first decade of this century, that number jumped to 83. Nearly half of the two billion people now getting by on between $10 and $100 a day – the global middle class – live in what the OECD calls "converging economies". (That is, economies that are catching up with the living standards of the West from a low base via turbo-charged growth.)

This has profound implications for global business. So do the massive demographic changes that are already under way around the world.

By 2050, other things being equal, there will be almost as many people in Nigeria as in America; Ethiopia will have twice as many people as Britain or Germany. But the working population of Japan and Russia could fall by roughly one-third over the same period.

The opportunities that all this throws up for business will not be evenly dispersed. Successful leaders of the future will need judgment, imagination and the capacity to work in unfamiliar surroundings if they are to make the most of these extraordinary shifts in global power balances.

In addition, our understanding of globalisation is becoming much more subtle and nuanced than was the case in an America-centric world. We are moving away from the simplistic notion that the world is flat towards a much more complex reality.

That is what today's business graduates need to understand. And to do that they will have to learn to live with and welcome diversity in all its forms. It is going to take a different kind of mindset, and a different type of education, to survive and prosper in such a diverse and cosmopolitan environment.

83

During the 1990s, just 12 countries in the world generated growth in incomes per head at a pace that was twice the OECD average. In the first decade of this century, that number jumped to 83

The great moderation is now well and truly over. The probability is that we will see much more jagged economic cycles in the next two decades than we saw in the last. And today's economic uncertainties are on a scale not seen since the second world war. Consider the euro crisis. The chances of a disorderly breakdown are small but not negligible. But the consequences of such an event would be catastrophic. The euro and the dollar together are the essential lubricants of global trade and finance, accounting for nearly two-thirds of trading in foreign exchange markets worldwide. That is one reason why the result of a euro collapse would be all but unimaginable.

The other is the potential impact on the global banking system at a time when the balance sheets of the world's big banks are so closely intertwined. To take one example, Britain's banks are not directly very vulnerable to the banking problems of Greece. But they are heavily exposed to those in France and Germany, which are. All this uncertainty helps to explain why companies in the developed world are building up vast cash mountains rather than investing their money in new products and services.

Dealing with uncertainty

The second great quality required of tomorrow's business leaders is the capacity to deal with uncertainty. This did not seem so necessary in the 15 years leading up to the latest financial crash – the period economists describe as "the great moderation", when inflation stayed low, asset prices rose and economies grew steadily just about everywhere. The Cold War was over, the Washington consensus shaped the world economy and the business outlook often appeared as assured as it was predictable.

Nor was uncertainty high on the agenda of most business schools. They were busy promoting the notion of rational economic man and the certainty of modern finance theory and economic modelling. Then things changed.

Since the credit crunch started in 2007, American non-financial companies have increased the share of their assets held in cash by 50% to around $1.7 trillion. Apple alone has almost $100 billion in the bank – enough to buy Dell three times over. Understandable, perhaps, but is it wise? Would bolder visionaries see today's uncertainty as an opportunity, rather than a risk? Think of the great businesses that have been created at the bottom of past economic cycles. Can business schools help business to think through this challenge?

The role of government

The third important quality that will be required of tomorrow's business leaders is a proper understanding of the role and workings of government.

Again, this seemed irrelevant during the period of the great moderation. The Reagan/Thatcher reforms had swept away corporatism and the heavy hand of the state and left market forces to do their work. As time passed, it came to seem – at least in the advanced economies – that almost any government interference in the workings of the market was likely to do damage. Now we had once again to learn the old lesson – that markets sometimes fail and that when they do governments have to step in. The British government had to save the country's banking system. The American government – and you have to pinch yourselves when you say this – had to nationalise General Motors, albeit briefly.

Across the whole of the developed world, governments are working on

major programmes of new legislation covering the financial system. Energy is another sector coming in for a wave of re-regulation. There are others.

Is this a temporary blip in the workings of free markets? Are we heading back to business as usual, when markets rule and governments only have a bit part to play? Or is the shock of the past few years going to change the way the global economy is managed in some fundamental way? Around the world, we see the growing reach of state-directed capitalism, most obviously in China, but also visible in Russia, Malaysia, Venezuela and elsewhere. According to the *Economist* magazine, state-backed companies today account for four-fifths of China's stock market and two-thirds of Russia's.

The world's ten biggest oil and gas firms, measured by reserves, are all state-owned. And as this form of enterprise advances we see a corresponding loss of confidence in the Anglo-American economic model.

The Occupy Wall Street camps, in their different manifestations around the world, are a small and largely incoherent protest movement. But I think they are a symptom of a broader malaise: a sense that something is not quite right in a world where the average income of the richest 10% of the population in advanced economies is now about nine times that of the poorest 10%. The spread is much steeper than that in countries such as America and Britain. And even in raditionally egalitarian societies, such as Germany, Denmark and Sweden, the income gap is expanding – from 5 to 1 in the 1980s to 6 to 1 today.

50%

Since the credit crunch started in 2007, American non-financial companies have increased the share of their assets held in cash by 50% to around $1.7 trillion. Apple alone has almost $100 billion in the bank – enough to buy Dell three times over

" *The world's ten biggest oil and gas firms, measured by reserves, are all state-owned. And as this form of enterprise advances we see a corresponding loss of confidence in the Anglo-American economic model*

The purpose of business

And so finally to the fourth quality, which is a developed understanding of the role, responsibilities and purposes of business itself.

Here again there is at least a chance that we are approaching a secular and not just a cyclical change in the way this subject is best approached – one that business schools, both in their roles as teachers and thought leaders, ought to be debating and leading. Business management in the decades after the second world war was shaped by what I think of as the Peter Drucker or Dave Packard approach.

The purpose of business was to meet the needs of customers. Firms had to make enough profits to undertake the research and marketing and to retain and develop the talented employees that were required to do a good job for their customers but no more than that. They did not exist for their own sake nor just to maximise their profits. Instead, they were a means to a broader end and they had a real interest in the wellbeing of the different communities that were touched by their activities.

Drucker himself forecast that this benign model would eventually collapse under the weight of two developments:

the rise of globalisation and of the hostile takeover. And of course he was right. Gradually, and then with increasing momentum, shareholder value became the driving force of business management, and business schools played an important part in pushing the process on. It brought real benefits, by driving out cost and inefficiencies and focusing on comparative advantage.

Consumers were big winners, as globalisation multiplied the choice and slashed the cost of a whole range of products and services. But there were costs, too. Long-term investment became harder to justify as shareholders' engagement became increasingly short term. Managers were heavily incentivised to maximise the returns on equity rather than on overall capital employed – one of the prime explanations for the banking crash. Companies became detached from their communities, as they shifted their activities to wherever in the world the job could be efficiently completed at the lowest price.

If the return on equity stacked up, actions were justified which would not have made sense in Drucker's world. And people paid a price. We all paid a lot less for our trousers, for our television sets and for our travel services. But the price was rising job insecurity and growing income inequality across the whole of the developed world. And after the economic shock of the past four years, we again have to ask the question: what is business actually for?

And what is the sensible response on the part of business to the largely hostile way in which the public debate is now being framed? In *Rethinking the MBA*, three Harvard Business School professors argue that one thing lacking in many MBA programmes is an understanding of how to balance

financial and non-financial objectives while simultaneously juggling the demands of diverse constituencies such as shareholders, employees, customers, regulators and society at large. That is surely correct.

Public concern about high levels of executive compensation, accounting irregularities, and flawed decision making have prompted considerable soul searching at business schools, driven in part by student pressure to have environmental, ethical and corporate responsibility issues embedded in the curriculum.

It is good that business school graduates are rising to this big challenge. But I think academics themselves should be doing more to shape the debate, through their research and their writings.

Today's business leaders are in a difficult place. They are being criticised for their lack of diversity and for their compensation practices. They rank close to the bottom of the opinion polls when it comes to questions of trust and reputation. After everything that has happened in the past few years, shareholder value no longer seems a reliable model on which to build a company's future. And they do not quite know how to handle the politics of a much more uncertain world.

They need guidance. They need big new ideas and fresh thinking about their role and responsibilities. And that, above everything else, is what business schools should be seeking to develop and promulgate today. **gf**

This article is an edited version of the presentation by Richard Lambert to the EFMD Meeting for Deans and Directors General, Nottingham Business School, February 2012

ABOUT THE AUTHOR
Sir Richard Lambert is Chancellor of Warwick University in Britain. He was editor of the *Financial Times* from 1991 to 2001, served on the Bank Of England Monetary Policy Committee 2003 to 2006 and was Director of the Confederation of British Industry 2006 to 2011. He also chaired the *Lambert Review* on the relationship between higher education and business.

gf

Section_01
The Purpose and Vision of a Business School

"The 'FT' ranking measures three main criteria: the career progression of graduates; the international focus of a programme; and the research capabilities of a business school"

George Bickerstaffe
'Top Rank Della Bradshaw Interview'

 Audio version

Volume

Issue

03_01

2009

The Financial Times's Della Bradshaw tells
George Bickerstaffe that people need to be
more relaxed about business school rankings

Top
Rank

" *The idea behind the FT rankings is to produce a listing of business schools around the world that are producing global managers for the 21st century*

She has been called the most important woman in management education – and occasionally other, much less flattering, things.

Della Bradshaw, Business Education Editor of the *Financial Times* in London and for the past ten years overseer of the newspaper's business school ranking system, is unimpressed by either approach.

The first makes her guffaw with laughter and the second to shrug, suggesting that business schools that react negatively are usually those that actively use their ranking position in their own promotional material.

Ms Bradshaw takes a down-to earth approach to her job that reflects her Yorkshire background (she was born in Leeds) tempered with a mischievous streak, laughing again when she is reminded of once saying that she was amazed that anyone took business school rankings seriously.

"Well I am a Brit," she says, as if that explains everything. "But perhaps it's not so much taking them seriously as a lack of context in how you see rankings. There's a lot more information available now on websites and so on than there was ten years ago and while rankings have a place and have always had a place I think people should take a more rounded view."

Certainly, though, the rankings themselves are taken extremely seriously by Ms Bradshaw and her team at the *FT*. The first ranking was launched in 1999 and ranked 50 business schools on the basis of their full-time MBA programmes.

An initial ranking the previous year was not used because Ms Bradshaw felt the methodology being used was "too biased"; in particular an attempt to include the views of MBA recruiters was not successful.

The idea behind the ranking, according to Ms Bradshaw, was – and still is – to produce a listing of business schools around the world that are producing global managers for the 21st century.

The *FT* ranking measures three main criteria: the career progression of graduates; the international focus of a programme; and the research capabilities of a business school.

The reasons the *Financial Times* decided to get involved in ranking appear complicated.

Certainly the then editor, Richard Lambert (now director-general of the Confederation of British Industry), was keen on the idea and it was something the newspaper believed it could do well.

There was also a certain amount of interest from schools in Europe, especially leading ones, who felt that they missed out on existing rankings (particularly in North America and particularly in *Business Week* magazine), which concentrated almost exclusively on American schools.

"It was driven by these two things," says Ms Bradshaw, "the *FT* feeling that this was something we could do and European schools wanting something that put them on a global stage."

The methodology for the rankings was developed in-house using the *FT*'s own research resources (of which it has a lot) plus a panel of eight business school representatives (four from European schools and four from America) to offer advice and suggestions.

"Some good ideas did come out of that but we also did some things that weren't suggested by them," comments Ms Bradshaw.

1999

The first ranking was launched
in 1999 and ranked 50 business
schools on the basis of their
full-time MBA programmes

Somewhat controversially at the time, though the idea has since been followed by others, the ranking also attempted to measure the research capabilities of business schools because "we wanted to find out where the new ideas were coming from".

The methodology for assessing this has evolved over time and is currently based on faculty publications in 40 selected academic journals.

Ms Bradshaw is well aware of the current debate about the relevance or otherwise of academic research into management and business, as displayed not least in the pages of *Global Focus*.

Couldn't she include some criteria that would include more practitioner-based research?

"Well we would like to have practitioner journals – but there aren't any," she says. "Practitioners don't want to read that stuff. That's the dilemma we are in."

Though often revered and reviled in equal measure by their world, she remains a firm fan of both business school academics and their students.

"I think you can learn new things from them [academics] that you never get from other people you might meet as a journalist," she says. "They really are people who have thought deeply about things. And there's an enthusiasm about MBA students that I really like."

Ms Bradshaw does not have an MBA or other management or business qualification herself but has "quite a good" degree in English from the University of Ulster in Northern Ireland where she studied from the early to mid-1970s – at the height of the sectarian "troubles", as she notes wryly.

Following graduation she taught English in Sicily, Turkey and Japan returning to Britain to write for

Electronics Weekly, a trade newspaper, and then joining the *Financial Times* as a technology writer. After maternity leave she returned to the *FT* to launch its business education page in 1995.

(Ms Bradshaw is married to fellow journalist Philip Beresford, another inveterate list-maker, who compiles, among other things, the annual "Rich List" of the British wealthy in the *Sunday Times* newspaper.)

During her time at the *FT* she has been a front-seat observer of some of the major changes in the world of business and management education.

Most significant, she believes has been the relative decline of the American market. Its former dominance has been challenged by the rising numbers and quality of business schools and programmes around the world, she says.

Also important, Ms Bradshaw says, has been the growing diversity of academic programmes offered by business schools, particularly the rise of specialised masters programmes in areas such as finance and pre-experience masters in management programmes.

This is reflected in the rankings now carried out by the *Financial Times*, which now include separate rankings for MBA, Executive MBA, European masters in management, European business schools and executive education.

Though open to the criticism often levelled at rankings, overall she believes they have had a positive effect on business schools and management education generally.

"I compare them to restaurant reviews," she says. "People tend to stick to a favourite reviewer and I think the rankings are bit like that. In America, schools tend to concentrate on *Business Week*.

> " "
> *In a business school faculty are obviously important but there are also other factors. The career development department in a business school is clearly critical*

8

The methodology for the rankings was developed in-house using the *FT*'s own research resources plus a panel of eight business school representatives – four from Europe, four from America

Outside America it's more likely to be the *FT* or the Economist Intelligence Unit."

Ms Bradshaw agrees, though, that rankings often measure very small differences between schools. That, she thinks, is inevitable.

"There are always going to be lots of schools that are very similar," she says. "In countries like Britain, where you have a lot of state-funded universities, that is always going to be the case. They will all be on much the same level. And I think the same is true of most European countries. That's where it becomes difficult. That's where they are likely to move about [in the rankings] depending on various factors."

What happens in rankings, she says, is that while each school is given a an individual place in the ranking, in effect the list is made up of several clusters of schools with similar scores but relatively large gaps between the clusters, especially at the top.

"What you find is that the top schools in all our rankings are way ahead of the rest," she says.

She also points out that ranking business schools is a multi-faceted business.

"I think that what you measure in a business school is different to what you would measure in any other university department," she says. "For example, a French department is only as good as its faculty.

"In a business school faculty are obviously important but there are also other factors. The career development department in a business school is clearly critical. People go to business school to get a better job. You don't study French to get a better job, it's more about pure education."

Ms Bradshaw does not foresee any major changes to the ranking in the *Financial Times* in the future. She thinks they will remain more or less the same, building on what already exists.

But, returning to her main theme she emphasises the need to keep the rankings in perspective, to look at them in a little more of a relaxed light.

"In some ways I think applicants should be a bit more intelligent rather than just rely entirely on rankings," she grins.

ABOUT THE AUTHOR

George Bickerstaffe is Consultant Editor of *Global Focus* and a consultant to CEEMAN. He is also author of *Which MBA?* which includes the annual Economist Intelligence Unit ranking of full-time MBA programmes. He has worked for the *Financial Times* in London, including contributing to the management education page.

Section_01
The Purpose and Vision of a Business School

"If the business school community wants to stay connected and exercise influence on the way our community is managed – and after all their core business is educating managers – then it is essential that they are outward looking and heard in society"

Gerard van Schaik
'Can business schools rescue business?'

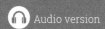 Audio version

Volume   Issue

03_03

gf

2009

Can business schools rescue business?

Did business schools cause the economic crisis?
No, says **Gerard van Schaik**, but they have a key
role in determining what comes next

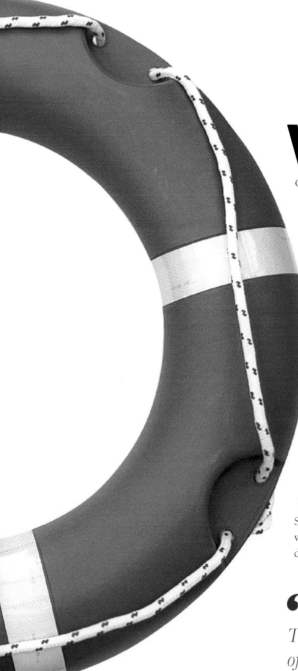

We are in a global economic mess and we know it is man-made. If we want to get out of the present chaos we will have to manage it ourselves; nature will not do it for us.

Crises come and crises go and during any period of insecurity there is invariably an outcry for "change"; change to the law, the rules, the system, our behaviour – you name it.

From all quarters of society come suggestions for what should be done to lead us back to our previous affluence and success.

We see a lot of opportunistic patchwork, not well thought-through legislation, regulation and restructuring. There is a lot of "quick fixing" done so change will mostly be superficial and of a temporary nature.

Having spent my active life in the corporate world I dare to say that approach is partly explained by the fact that line managers – who take the operational steps in organisations – are in general quickly bored with lengthy analyses and time-consuming research.

Moreover, the present generation of managers has been educated to act fast, to "diagnose and cure" quickly using sophisticated toolkits and is conditioned to go for optimal results (both for the business and for themselves) in the shortest period of time.

The call for change is also heard in the world of business education. Business schools ask themselves what the impact of the ongoing crisis is on their own future and the products they bring to market.

Self-reflection is positive. It is very necessary that the academic world looks hard at what it is doing from time to time and probes whether there is cause for revision or drastic overhaul of programmes.

""

The relationships that are cemented with students of executive development programmes should be used to exchange mutual experience, knowledge and research to discover how the spectrum of the school can be widened and its role in the business world can be enhanced

I am convinced, however, that the outcome of this process will not be that the knowledge and skills acquired at business schools inevitably produce managers who are doomed to create the type of mess we are now in. Fortunately, we know that is nonsense. If it were not we would be in a sorry state and schools would have a serious problem.

Much of what has happened in the recent past has to do with dishonesty and immorality. Business schools cannot be blamed for unknowingly having trained and educated a limited number of crooks among tens of thousands of honest, incorruptible managers.

What they could ask themselves, however, is whether they are inclined to sometimes too easily accept as a given the business fads and fashions of the day . Indeed, they may even wonder if they actually help to develop them further without properly researching where it might ultimately lead. Taking the recent past, one can think of such trends as shareholder focus, reward systems, financial product development and others.

I am not in a position to judge what action business schools should take to better serve their customers (their customers being society as whole not just their students) in years to come. I feel that reputable schools around the world have served business and public institutions well in the past and supplied the type of managers business asked for.

The crazy excesses that we saw (and still see in some quarters) in management behaviour such as large scale-fraud, environmental crime, exhibitionistic remuneration and so on are not the product of management education but of the business community itself.

If you introduce business philosophies that focus on short-term gain and then link them to pay packets that benefit from inflating financial results you should not be surprised that some characters will use every trick in the book to foster their own wealth. If social control on such behaviour is virtually non-existent it is just a matter of time before things blow up in your face. Codes, rules and regulations may make it more difficult in future for people to behave excessively in this respect but will not prevent it.

During the last decade the shareholder was the idol that had to be served unconditionally as the sole owner of the corporation. Although this is legally true, we all knew that with this approach business created its own problems.

The shareholder is the least faithful of stakeholders in a company and are in nine out of 10 cases corporations or institutions that strive to maximise their own profits. They are interested in share value and dividend and not in the market position or strategic direction of a company they invest in. If they can do a better deal somewhere else they move out, not caring a dime what the long-term consequences are for the corporation when they say goodbye to it.

Although the negatives of abandoning the stakeholder approach and the beatification of the shareholder were already publicly noted in the early 1990s it took two crises before the focus on stakeholders – shareholders being one

> *If one wants to judge the role of business education in these developments one can ask the question whether business schools have been close enough to their customers to be able to influence or criticise thinking or have they limited themselves solely to their student body?*

of them – was actively reintroduced in business schools.

In 2000 the concept of global social responsibility was launched, highlighting the fact that the manager of the future would have to consider the strategies and actions of his or her corporation or division in a societal context and not only on a company or industry basis.

We are almost 10 years down the road and we are still discussing how the idea should be made operational both in teaching programmes and at a corporate level so that it does not become just a "show" chapter but an integral part of the business plan.

Although it is now – thanks to the crisis – generally accepted that social responsibility is a core focal point in business a great number of business schools seem to have missed an opportunity to take a lead by being too slow on the uptake.

Business life has always known many "fads". In my active corporate life we have had the period in which production was core, then marketing, financial control, logistics, human resources – each discipline got its turn in prominence. Consultants and business schools were quite often the instigators of the temporary focus on a certain discipline. But at a certain moment the financial discipline started to overshadow everything. In the process

2000

The year the concept of global social responsibility was launched, highlighting the fact that the manager of the future would have to consider the strategies and actions of his or her corporation or division in a societal context

corporate "money"became an "objective" instead of a "means" and it still is.

If one wants to judge the role of business education in these developments one can ask the question whether business schools have been close enough to their customers to be able to influence or criticise thinking or have they limited themselves solely to their student body? Have they tried to be a counterweight in situations where in their view corporate policies and government actions in general were to the detriment of the long-term welfare of society and the business community?

Most people would say this is not the mission of a business school. It should just deliver well-trained managers who are sensitive of the place in society of the entity they are serving.

I think the latter view is narrowing the field of responsibility of a business school too much.

But how far the business school community should go in trying to participate actively in the operational implementation of the social responsibility concept in the corporation or a public institution is for me an open question. I think they should try to play some role in future through some form of partnership but research will have to help us find out whether such a thing is possible and desirable.

" "

Business schools have a lot to offer through their international networks, their experience with people from different occupations and different cultures and their expertise in enhancing the "quality" of people

One thing that this crisis is making abundantly clear is the question of whether the business school community (as part of our society) should play a more missionary and a more pro-active role in future. Should it play a "guiding" function with regard to the do's and don'ts in the business community? I think so.

Business schools have a lot to offer through their international networks, their experience with people from different occupations and different cultures and their expertise in enhancing the "quality" of people. Apart from the many other channels through which they can make their views known, their executive education programmes give them a direct link to a variety of businesses and they should capitalise on this.

These contacts should be exploited to see what's brewing in society, what new ideas and approaches are developing in the business world, and try to play a role in the discussion. The relationships that are cemented with students of executive development programmes should be used to exchange mutual experience, knowledge and research to discover how the spectrum of the school can be widened and its role in the business world can be enhanced.

If the business school community wants to stay connected and exercise influence on the way our community is managed – and after all their core business is educating managers – then it is essential that they are outward looking and heard in society.

In the world of business and government no-one cares how business schools are organised internally, whether they publish sufficient articles in reputable journals, what liaisons they have and what research is being done. That's their problem.

The outside world is only interested in the variety and quality of the products they offer, the quality of their graduates and their contribution to society. The present crisis has highlighted that there is ample room and reason to play a role in the debate on how businesses should be restructured and run during and after the economic recovery.

There is no doubt in my mind, though, that in spite of all the indignation about moral excesses and the calls for change the moment the economy really picks up again most of that will be forgotten. The corporate world will continue restructuring and control the development of costs but will be busy again with its day-to-day worries and, apart from isolated cases, little if any fundamental change will take place in society.

If we are not careful, steps taken in the field of social responsibility at the company level may drop out of the system and we will chase profits and bonuses in the way we used to.

So now is the time to make it abundantly clear that management as before is no longer acceptable. We want to ensure that the view that the company is part of society and has responsibilities to society at large is preserved. It cannot just consider the interest of its own industry or a limited number of stakeholders.

Business schools have a role to play here. They educate the future generation of managers and can convince them that by managing differently to their predecessors they can secure both the continuity of their business and the trust of society.

We should avoid at all costs governments telling us how we should run our businesses, though the present situation may be tempting for them.

This means: taking the company out of its isolation and putting it slam in the middle of society; demonstrating that by managing a company in a socially responsible way you can still maximise profits, and can still contribute to the welfare of interested parties but also to society at large thus winning the trust and acceptance of the general public and securing the continuity of your business.

Many things need to be revisited in the programmes that are being taught in business schools if we want to take into account the things we learn from the chaos we are in. But little of it has to do with management techniques. It is more a matter of bringing soft skills more to the fore and emphasising which things are relevant in managing and running a company or an institution that cannot be worked out on a computer.

It is desirable that in the rethinking process that will take place in the business school world creative thinking will dominate and that the "soft" side of business will not be caught and taught in rigid formats but with adequate room for cultural differences and personal convictions .

After all, techniques are a help but ultimately you manage with your guts. Now more than ever.

Whatever is revisited it is to be hoped that the end result will make business schools more outward looking than ever before, will bring them in permanent close working contact with their market (business or government) and make sure their views are heard in society. **gf**

ABOUT THE AUTHOR
Gerard van Schaik is Honorary President of EFMD, Former EFMD President and Former Chairman of the Executive Board of Heineken NV.

gf

Section_01
The Purpose and Vision of a Business School

"Universities are entrusted with the public duty of education. We contribute towards the greater good of the global economy and wider society by enriching, shaping and transforming students who will go on to make a difference in society"

Arnoud De Meyer
'Transforming business schools into 'Schools for Business''

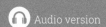 Audio version

Volume   Issue

05_03

gf

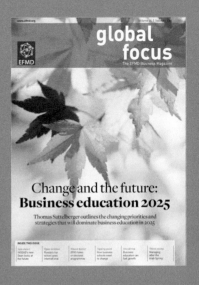

2011

Does the DNA of Business Schools need to change?

Arnoud De Meyer argues for a new approach to meet new challenges – transforming business schools into 'Schools for Business'

The last ten years have been a golden era for business schools. But I am convinced we have reached a watershed.

Business schools were content with a narrow focus defined by traditional management disciplines. Our attitude was that we as business schools knew "what was good for you".

Is this model of education inadequate for the realities of today's global economy? Just look at the challenges and problems of the world today: the rash of violent uprisings in the Middle East threatening to bring down powerful strongholds; natural calamities rendering nations powerless; Wikileaks causing embarrassment to government leaders; and the ripple of financial catastrophes tearing institutions apart and exposing corporate malfeasance.

The causes, effects and consequences concern corporate governance and organisational management as much as political conflict, environmental sustainability and foreign diplomacy.

These challenges cannot be addressed by the traditional management disciplines alone. They require fresh eyes looking through multi-disciplinary lenses beyond just management. To do this effectively, business schools need to bring onboard scholars and experts in political science, sociology, nuclear physics, ethics and morality, technology, national security and engineering sciences.

It is becoming imperative for business schools to develop a body of research and teaching capabilities that are able to address the systemic problems of the world today in a holistic, inter-disciplinary way. The world of business, government and non-profits are increasingly calling upon experts in

academia to find integrated solutions to their complex issues. This is the new challenge.

In *Business Schools on an Innovation Mission*, a report released by the Association to Advance Collegiate Schools of Business (AACSB) in May 2010, management and leadership were clearly positioned, side-by-side with science and technology, as vital components to the innovation value chain.

The report goes on to say that one aspect of innovation is for business schools to promote inter-disciplinary research by breaking down functional silos and disciplinary barriers in learning and research. I am in full agreement with this.

This brings me to my key message: business schools need to become "Schools for Business".

This is a paradigm shift for the world's business schools, a tipping point that can become a quantum leap if scholars and researchers are brave enough to break out of their comfort zones, combine their arsenal of expertise and confidently propose analysis, insights and solutions on a *smorgasbord* of issues that confront organisations across multiple disciplines.

Does this mean specialised, discipline-based research is no longer important? Absolutely not. Business schools still need to build up their core strengths in rigorous academic research in order to have the foundation to drive inter-disciplinary research and teaching.

Only then can they be of value and able to impart knowledge and skills to business leaders, helping them to advance their organisations, create positive social change and a better quality of life for their communities.

Over the last ten years, we at the Singapore Management University (SMU) have built up a body of high-quality, leading-edge research that is relevant and responsive to the needs of society, especially Asian issues with global impact.

At the same time, SMU has anchored itself in a distinctive brand of holistic, broad-based education aimed at producing creative and entrepreneurial leaders for the knowledge-based economy.

||||||||||||||||||||||||||||||||||||||||||||||||||||||||

"

This is a paradigm shift for the world's business schools, a tipping point that can become a quantum leap if scholars and researchers are brave enough

The business world exists as an eco-system of business, government, NGOs and non-profits, each interlocking with the other. This is also why research has to be inter-disciplinary, to consider the impact across different stakeholders.

With six schools covering the spectrum of accountancy, business, economics, information systems, law and social sciences, SMU is able to integrate the necessary elements across different disciplines to help governments and businesses solve practical problems. Being young and not burdened by legacy, this has been SMU's advantage in building up inter-disciplinary research and education.

To be truly a "School for Business" it is also important to build strong relationships and strategic partnerships with the business world. In its short ten-year history, SMU has forged close ties with major industry stakeholders through internships, executive education, postgraduate studies, research centres and institutes, corporate social responsibility and philanthropic partnerships.

The university has held steadfast to its mission of integrating the two worlds of education and business, sharing the wealth of knowledge with the business world and bringing industry wisdom into the halls of academia.

SMU has 19 research centres and institutes that bridge academia and business. These were formed through partnerships and collaborations with leading business organisations and institutions. Tapping the pulse of the latest market trends, they carry out research on most current issues and share the outcomes with business leaders. I will just share a few examples.

The university's Sim Kee Boon Institute for Financial Economics is a specialised think-tank that carries out research across financial econometrics, the impact of ageing populations on retirement funds, corporate and investor responsibility, asset securitisation and management in Asia.

Last year, three SMU faculty from different disciplines – finance, economics and information systems – carried out a collaborated study of the "Flash Crash", which took place in New York on May 6, 2010. Sponsored by the Institute for Financial Markets in Washington DC, the study deployed complex system research to conduct a market simulation, understand the causes behind it and recommend possible interventions.

The Institute of Service Excellence is involved in a number of inter-disciplinary projects. The institute, which is rooted in marketing research and expertise in customer satisfaction benchmarking, has invited researchers in organisational behaviour and human resources to develop a new structural model to measure fair dealing in financial institutions when they conduct business with customers such as financial advisory services and selling investment products and services. The institute has also collaborated with faculty in information systems to study the relationship between IT innovations and

" "
Leadership has evolved from the days of traditional 'command and control' to today's collaborative leadership, which suits present business climates better

customer experience in large organisations. The SMU-Carnegie Mellon Living Analytics Research Centre, the newest addition to the slate of research centres and institutes, is in the middle of a study on social media by applying management science concepts to predict trust and relationships among members of the online community such as product reviewers on Epinions, and buyers and sellers over eBay. The study involves researchers in three distinct areas: information systems, sociology and organisational behaviour and human resources.

Moving on to teaching, we know that business schools (and their MBA programmes) are largely about leadership development. We are preparing graduates to take on leadership positions in the business world.

Leadership has, however, evolved from the days of traditional "command and control" to today's collaborative leadership, which suits present business climates better. Leaders are now expected to have skills in collaboration, listening, influencing and flexible adaptation. How can business schools impart such qualities? One way is to ensure that students are well anchored in their area of expertise but also sufficiently exposed to wider disciplines outside their scope of specialisation.

SMU embraces this in our undergraduate curriculum. Every freshman takes a bundle of diverse courses as part of the University Core to develop essential skills in analytical and creative thinking, communication, leadership and teambuilding, ethics and social responsibility, and understanding the relationship between business, government and society in the context of world developments.

As they go on to specialise, a wide range of electives in the arts and sciences are available to broaden their perspectives and expose them to areas beyond their disciplines. These include courses in European languages, Shakespeare, film, dance, theatre, entertainment industries, environmental science, biotechnology and bio-entrepreneurship.

We believe a broad-based exposure makes students much more versatile, open-minded, people-sensitive and adept in real-world problem solving.

Inter-disciplinary teaching is helped, to a great extent, by having SMU's business school within a larger university for the world of business and management.

As businesses struggle to put in place measures to address gaps in governance and regulation in the wake of corporate scandals, universities can play a part by inculcating the right values through character building.

Universities are entrusted with the public duty of education. We contribute towards the greater good of the global economy and wider society by enriching, shaping and transforming students who will go on to make a difference in society. This is a role we need to discharge conscientiously. **gf**

19

SMU has 19 research centres and institutes that bridge academia and business, formed through partnerships and collaborations with leading business organisations and institutions

ABOUT THE AUTHOR
Professor Arnoud De Meyer is President,
Singapore Management University

Section_01
The Purpose and Vision of a Business School

"The challenge for schools that want to survive is redefining what a quality business school looks like. There are likely to be various models of this, but it is our belief that one of the qualities they will have in common is an emphasis on value creation that speaks to both our economic and our social needs"

Ken Starkey and Howard Thomas
'The future of business schools:
shut them down or broaden our horizons?'

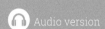 Audio version

Volume   Issue

13_02

2019

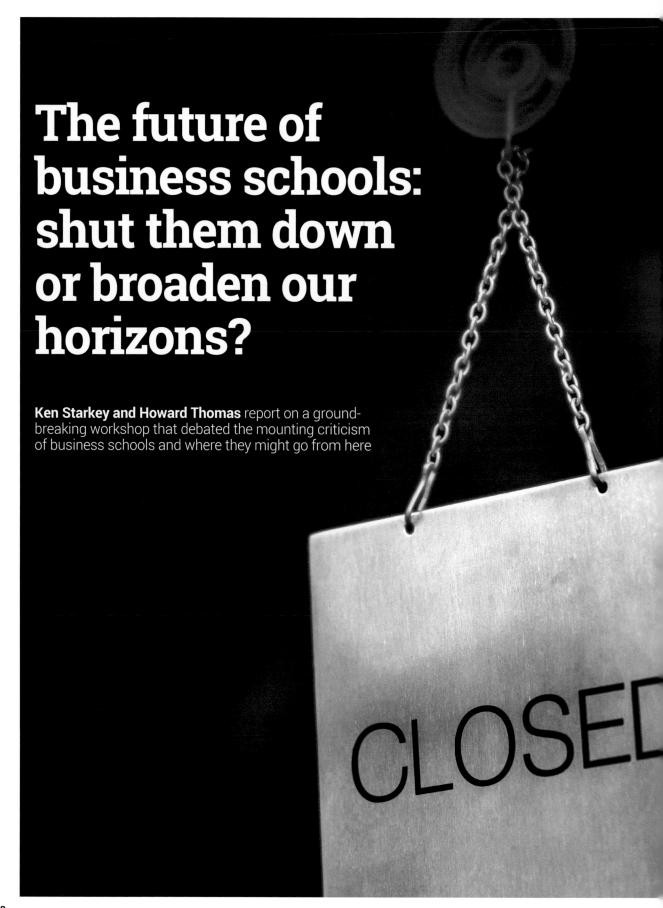

The future of business schools: shut them down or broaden our horizons?

Ken Starkey and Howard Thomas report on a ground-breaking workshop that debated the mounting criticism of business schools and where they might go from here

Inequality and austerity regimes are persistent reminders of a financial crisis brought on by particular practices of management

We live in turbulent and complicated times and business schools are not immune to the uncertainties that now afflict so many aspects of our social and economic lives. The quality of today's leaders poses some serious philosophical and strategic questions for business schools such as what are we, what do we want to be, should we be satisfied with what we are?

Top business schools often describe their mission as educating leaders yet many think that the world is currently experiencing a crisis of leadership that has helped create our current problems. The students we educate, particularly MBAs, accountants and finance professionals, are implicated in current criticisms of corporate behaviour.

We hear criticisms of globalisation (by, for example, a US President educated at one of the world's leading business schools). Inequality and austerity regimes are persistent reminders of a financial crisis brought on by particular practices of management (for example, the use of leverage), endorsed in the research and teaching of top business schools.

Perhaps the critics of business schools are correct and we are not fit for purpose. A much-discussed recent criticism was that of UK business school professor, Martin Parker (2018). His book, *Shut Down the Business School: What's Wrong with Management Education* (Pluto Press), was written from a European (particularly UK) perspective. Alongside such well-known writers as Henry Mintzberg, he argues that business school education is framed in terms of a winner-takes-all managerialism.

Students are taught that the purpose of management is to promote market values and to maximise their returns at the expense of others. Human resource management theory suggests that human beings are no more than rational egoists seeking to maximise their own interests by developing their human capital. Marketing teaches how to manipulate consumer desire. If we are judged by the current standing of business and the quality of business leadership then, as Parker suggests, we have questions to answer.

Parker's is a vigorous and entertaining restatement of criticism that has been voiced before, perhaps most convincingly by Harvard Business School's Rakesh Khurana (2007) in his institutional history of the evolution and transformation of US business schools *(From Higher Aims to Hired Hands: The Social Transformation of American Business Schools* and the *Unfulfilled Promise of Management as a Profession* (Princeton University Press).

Khurana's central argument is that business schools began with a great promise of contributing to public value through developing management as a profession. This promise was unfulfilled because business schools have become the hired hands of business and reneged on these higher aims. In essence they have sold out to the highest bidders.

In November 2018, the authors convened a workshop at Nottingham University Business School in the UK in collaboration with the Research Committee of EFMD to discuss such criticisms and to debate where business schools might go from here. The speakers at the seminar are listed on page 49 and this article summarises the debates at the workshop and sets out what we think are the urgent issues we need to address if we are to react proactively rather than defensively to criticism.

First, we have to recognise the truth of some of the criticisms of business schools. There is much in business that deserves condemnation and can be traced back to certain aspects and principles of management education that business schools have promulgated, some would say "indoctrinated", their students into. Indeed, the late Sumantra Ghoshal eloquently pointed out that teaching "amoral" theories led to questionable managerial practices that advocated shareholder value and profit maximisation over responsible corporate management.

Parker's positive contribution is that we need to shift our focus to new forms of management education, on different ways of organising to create outcomes for a broad range of stakeholders rather than just financial value for shareholders. As he also recommends closing down business schools, this work will need to be done in social science and humanities departments, which have the perspectives needed to help redefine business in terms of its broader potential contribution to value and society. We need a greater diversity of perspectives to improve/challenge what is in essence an "anglo-saxon" model of capitalism.

Of course, some business schools are already trying to achieve this and as Chinese schools mature they will, with due regard to their political masters, have to develop a different, more culturally contextual model. For the moment, though, schools that aspire to be "world class" have chosen to play a game defined by top US schools and embodied in league tables dominated by schools such as Harvard and Stanford.

The challenge is for business schools to reconceive their purpose, to reflect on the hegemony of management education rooted in the dominance of finance and economics, and to offer a new vision that helps define a cure for our current ills rather than contributing to their continuing effects.

This is vital in achieving a positive, more sustainable identity and legitimacy for the business school. It will also call into question the role that is frequently allocated to business schools of being a university's cash cow. In the

We need a greater diversity of perspectives to improve/challenge what is in essence an "anglo-saxon" model of capitalism

UK, this has reached epic proportions, leaving many wondering if their main role is to teach business English to Chinese students who represent a disproportionately large part of the UK postgraduate population.

China will not save us in the long term. Indeed, it might well be that in the fullness of time our complicity with the economic miracle of China comes to be seen as a major strategic mistake. We need to justify our existence and our role in more sustainable ways and with more of a local contextual regard. As Sue Cox reminded us, some business schools have an excellent story to tell in terms of their significant contributions to local and regional economies.

Business school faculty also need to reflect on the contribution they are supposedly making to business and society. For many faculty, the main focus of their existence is the search for the holy grail of publishing in A* journals.

This has become a major industry in its own right, prompted by the advent of the rankings era that shaped business schools as " businesses" with the rules of their game framed by the Gordon/Howell US studies.

Many now think there are too many business schools, too many students studying business and management, and too many journals publishing too much research, most of which is barely read except by a few other academics and has no impact whatsoever. The unpalatable truth

is that it is finance research that has really changed the world but only for the benefit of a minority. The impact of most management research is minimal.

We are complicit in creating a publishing system that serves our purposes but has very little value beyond that except for the journal publishers and for the minority who publish at the highest level. We produce case studies that are widely read and used in teaching but our case studies too often focus on fashionable companies that enjoy all too brief success, followed sometimes by spectacular falls from grace.

Enron, various dot.coms, Royal Bank of Scotland and now Facebook spring to mind. These are hardly examples that inspire much confidence in our ability to back winners that will change the world for the better!

Wallace Donham, the second Dean of Harvard Business School, during the depression of the 1930s, argued that business schools needed to broaden their horizon. They do not exist just for the benefit of an elite minority. They have the potential to make a broad contribution to the economy and society and, he argued, should think in terms of broad social problems and effective social systems instead of focusing only on individual companies. Sadly, his wise words did not change the trajectory of business school development.

However, there is emerging evidence in the US and the UK of a student shift from a sole focus on shareholder value to one on stakeholder value encompassing issues of sustainability, inequality and inclusive growth. This should certainly stimulate the creation of more balanced, holistic models of management education.

Donham's ideas are still very relevant to our current situation. Perhaps the most interesting example of how we might embed them in current business school practice was the argument by Martin Kitchener, former Dean of Cardiff University Business School in the UK, that our focus should be on creating "public value" business schools. As Cox reminded us, this will require critical dialogue with business and other stakeholders -- local, regional, national and international.

Kitchener argues that what we need is more imaginative and entrepreneurial business schools that combine four qualities: philosophical; political; managerial; and technical. These qualities give us a framework for analysing what we currently do, what we might want to do in future, and what we might have to do to survive and prosper when the business school gravy train hits the buffers at the end of its current line. It also gives us a basis for rethinking the current governance of business schools.

The public value business school concept gives us compelling alternatives to the current state in which we find ourselves. While unlikely to appeal to all, it has the capacity to help us redefine our purpose and for addressing the pervasive criticisms of business schools concerning their self-centred approach to knowledge creation, the particular values embedded in their teaching and their modes of engagement with stakeholders. As Julie Davies of Huddersfield Business School in the UK pointed out, it will require forging a new social contract with the communities we profess to serve and a new commitment to deliver public value social science.

To understand and prepare for the future of business schools and management education we need to understand better why we are where what we are and what we have become in the light of a history that possessed a number of alternative paths. The key message of our workshop was that we need to think critically about where we are and what we might become. We also need to recognise what he have lost in terms of pursuing a particular path that is embodied (some might say "embalmed") in leagues and ranking tables such as those of the *Financial Times* and *Business Week*.

In the end, while sensitive to some of Parker's criticisms, we were unwilling to follow him all the way to his conclusion that we needed to shut down the business schools. In our development, as Khurana points out, there has been much to praise and much promise. Our challenge is that much of the promise has not been fully realised and we are losing legitimacy as a result.

The choices we make in the next few years will have huge consequences -- for individual schools and for the very idea of what a business school is and might be. For example, as many have pointed out, it is important to recognise the global phenomenon and success of the undergraduate business programme and the relative inattention afforded it compared to the MBA in curriculum development.

Therefore, it was argued that renewed attention should be given to liberal education models. These propose that rather than focusing on specific management and technical skills there should be greater curriculum breadth with the humanities and the social sciences as a core foundation of learning in management education. This would enable students and faculty to converse in the great traditions of thought and expression before instruction in specific management training.

We suspect that market forces will inevitably lead to the closure of business schools. We cannot envisage more growth of the kind we have experienced over the last quarter of a century. The challenge for those schools that want to survive and prosper is redefining what a quality business school looks like. There are likely to be various models of this, national and international, but it is our belief that one of the qualities they will have in common is an emphasis on value creation that speaks to both our economic and our social needs.

On this positive and optimistic note, we will continue the discussion of how we might broaden our horizons at a series of follow on workshops during 2019/20. We believe that such discussions and collaboration in the areas of best teaching and research practices across schools will produce worthwhile dividends in the development of a stronger management education ecosystem, particularly in the UK but also across the rest of Europe. Please let us know what you think we need to discuss and if you would like to be involved.

About the Authors

Professor Ken Starkey graduated in modern languages and literature. He studied for a psychology degree while working as a Special Needs Teacher and worked as Research Fellow in the School of Modern Languages, Aston University, while pursuing a PhD. He joined the University of Nottingham in 1988 and is a professor at Nottingham University Business School.

Professor Howard Thomas is Emeritus Dean and LKCSB Distinguished Professor of Strategic Management, Lee Kong Chian School of Business, Singapore Management University. He is also He is also Visiting Professor of Global Leadership at the Questrom School of Business , Boston University, and also a Visiting Professor of Strategy at GIBS, South Africa, and Coventry University, UK.

List of seminar speakers

Martin Parker (Bristol University)
Sue Cox (Lancaster University)
Howard Thomas (EFMD, SMU, Boston University, Coventry University)
Ken Starkey (Nottingham University)
Julie Davies (Huddersfield University)
Simon Collinson (C-ABS, Birmingham University)
Sue Tempest (Nottingham University)

Section_02
Business Models and the Paradigm Trap

"The link between the business
and the academic worlds must
be strengthened and redesigned.
It is clear that there is a need for
a consultation process to discuss
the definition of strategic objectives
the development of shared
infrastructures, and the production
of competencies"

Eric Cornuel
'University challenge'

 Audio version

Volume   Issue

01_01

2007

> The greatest obstacle to proper resourcing seems to be that most European universities remain largely state-funded rather than having diversified sources of revenue

University challenge

ERIC CORNUEL, DIRECTOR GENERAL & CEO OF EFMD, ANALYSES THE COMPLEX ISSUES FACED BY EUROPE'S HIGHER EDUCATION SECTOR, PARTICULARLY BUSINESS SCHOOLS

The main goal of any higher education institution should be to deliver (and continually enhance) excellence in teaching and learning and to combine the values of a liberal education with the professional qualifications required in a global economy.

To achieve this, the successful business schools of the future will need to ensure an adequate level of resources to realise their mission statements and recruit qualified faculty. They will need adequately funded doctoral research programmes and other incentives for academics. They will need to globalise not just their faculty and student body but also their curricula (which will have to be re-shaped to be both multicultural and multidisciplinary). And they will need to train students to become globally responsible leaders.

While these challenges are common to business schools worldwide, there is concern in Europe over the possible declining level of its higher education offerings. One element of worry comes from the great discrepancy in resources available to European universities when compared to those of their competitors. European business schools could quickly find themselves unable to recruit the same quality of researchers and faculty as their counterparts in America and elsewhere, spending less on research programmes and struggling to provide attractive offerings in a competitive market.

The greatest obstacle to proper resourcing seems to be that most European universities remain largely state-funded rather than having diversified sources of revenue (student fees, business and donors). Everywhere in Europe, with the notable exception of Scandinavia, budgets for higher education and research appear to be falling. In many cases the state even prohibits charging tuition fees and creates obstacles to the use of other sources of revenue.

With its low levels of funding, Europe may be less able to adapt to the changing needs and demands of the market and to adopt appropriate solutions for the challenges that business schools will face in the future.

Where is the faculty?

A large number of business schools are facing the problem of faculty shortages while demand for management education continues to grow. Customised programmes for companies, are one particular area where the customer is demanding a more personalised learning journey, while the provider is struggling to meet these expectations

which require the hiring of a considerable number of experienced faculty. Unless doctoral research and education in this field is encouraged, the level and perhaps even quality of business education offered worldwide will decrease and business schools will no longer be able to prepare future professionals and leaders for the global economy.

Within the next decade the US will have a predicted shortfall of 2,500 academics in management disciplines alone. Given the law of supply and demand, it becomes easy to see how this will translate into a significant acceleration in the movement of faculty westwards across the Atlantic.

This problem is even more acute in Europe, where it is again rooted in the lack of resources. European institutions will need to match the global salary levels of their competitors, particularly in America, if they are not to face serious problems. Young lecturers in quality business schools in America currently earn about €100,000 a year while in Europe the comparable figure is around €60,000.

It should, then, be of no surprise that of the 1,200 top scientists in the world, the great majority are in America, with only 80 in Britain, 65 in Germany and 30 in France. Furthermore, according to The Economist, 70% of the world's Nobel prize-winners are working for American universities; 30% of articles published on science and engineering, and almost half of the world's most-cited articles are produced there. Note that the greatest upcoming competitor in this field is China, which is attracting an increasing number of international faculty, and in particular American PhDs.

Some short-term solutions, such as hiring part-time faculty, academics from other disciplines, or retired business professionals, are open to business schools. But the problem needs be tackled at its roots: doctoral research in the management fields needs greater resources. Measures such as higher salaries and tax incentives should be provided to young students to encourage them to pursue an academic career in business and remain in the field.

One way to provide these extra resources might be the concept of academic clusters – cross-border alliances of academic institutions and business schools, a sort of academic Airbus. (It is frequently easier to be close friends with near neighbours than with immediate family!)

At present, many institutions are simply too small. Alliances – even mergers – would create the economies of scale necessary to fund the changes that business schools and universities need, as well as raise cross-border and multicultural awareness.

> Developing the competencies, capacities and attitudes required for the next generation of globally responsible leaders requires more than relying solely on the simple acquisition of knowledge

In a way, of course, this is yet another example of the pervasive globalisation of the management education sector, yet another of the key challenges business schools face.

The world on our doorstep

The globalisation of management education has a number of implications.

First, business school faculty itself must have a relevant international dimension (not just a different passport) that will transmit the benefits of global learning and experiences to its students.

Second, schools need to respond positively to the fact that their students are increasingly drawn from an international pool – the market for management education is a global one. If their student body is not international, then they should try to make it so.

Third, they must adapt and develop their curricula to reflect the global nature of business and the global factors impacting managers, whether or not they are so-called "international managers". The world is now so small and flat that every manager, whatever his or her role, is affected by the global nature of business.

Finally, they need to increase the global nature of their research. It is a sad fact that most research papers still focus on Western businesses. This can hinder the development of the international content of programmes and courses and, as a consequence, a global mindset in students. Research should also be more relevant, keeping in mind that the final goal is the improvement of management of an organisation.

Some business schools have made great strides in this area via, for example, the establishment of cross-cultural programme teams, regional and national campus days, exchange programmes with other business schools around the world, student visits to other countries, and projects and internships in locations outside their own region.

Curricula also need to be made more international in scope to broaden students' knowledge and awareness of non-Western business practices. The development and use of international case studies from around the world is one way to create familiarity with a wide range of countries and cultures. In addition, there needs to be a more equitable balance between the transfer of west-east and east-west knowledge, skills and attitudes.

In the corporate world, a number of businesses now offer business schools the opportunity for MBA and other students to visit or take up internships to build both a vision of corporate global responsibility and to gain international experience. Such opportunities should be encouraged – and increased.

In Europe, the Bologna process is proving an effective tool to promote and facilitate student mobility by harmonising academic degree standards and quality assurance standards throughout Europe. Schools need to be aware, though, that with students travelling across the continent in a more transparent system, competition will inevitably increase. Already 45 countries have signed the Bologna Accord, and many more are considering it. This is leading to the establishment of a common higher education area which was initiated and carried forward by Europe. This is a great step forward.

At the same time, curricula will have to be more "global" in the multidisciplinary sense. The job market will increasingly demand skills across a variety of fields and demand for joint studies such as business technology programmes will be high.

The reason is that managers in the future will not be able to compete just on the basis of a theoretical business degree, and this is because of many factors not just because of the influence of globalisation. They will need to acquire practical skills that will allow them to become – and manage – the knowledge workers of the future. Learning processes will have to become more real-world focused.

COURTESY: LONDON BUSINESS SCHOOL

70%
of the world's Nobel prize-winners are working for American universities

Changing the curriculum

One of the problems of management education remains its continuing (though reduced) emphasis on the trappings of functional disciplines when in reality managers work in a cross-disciplinary, even multidisciplinary, world. So many different elements interact each with the other that managers must be capable of a broader view.

Developing the competencies, capacities and attitudes required for the next generation of globally responsible leaders requires more than relying solely on the simple acquisition of knowledge. Experiential, presentational, propositional and practical ways of learning must be integrated into the curriculum.

The top business schools of the future will train their students to meet the demands of an increasingly complex world and in doing so they will use challenging and innovative approaches to management education. They will implement substantial changes in the ways they prepare the next generation of leaders.

In particular, I believe they will, and should, put globally responsible leadership and corporate responsibility at the heart of the business school curriculum. This will also present the schools with an opportunity to expand and enrich their academic offering and to employ new pedagogical approaches.

While some schools are already employing multidisciplinary approaches to learning, the topic of corporate global responsibility presents a further opportunity for integrated learning and for co-operation between traditional business school subject areas. Corporate global responsibility requires both the knowledge and application of learning to a diverse set of business topics. Studies in this area provide an avenue whereby business schools can move beyond functional boundaries to holistic practice.

We need to focus on leadership because too often today we encounter a management style that is somewhat harsh, that confronts people rather than supports them, that punishes them for mistakes and that focuses only on shareholder value. As a result, people are stressed and ill at ease in their work. I believe that we must encourage more human (and humane) values in management, especially forgiveness and health at work. Leadership training should aim at developing a style of management that promotes these values. If you do not forgive people for

> innovative programmes backed by the appropriate resources to guarantee an excellent faculty body, an international experience and a multicultural environment

Above
Professor Eric Cornuel

making mistakes, their confidence can easily be destroyed. If you forgive them, you give them a chance to learn and you earn legitimacy.

These values are very important if we wish to develop and retain people. Dedication and loyalty will be achieved only if this is done.

What next?

I believe that the successful business schools of the future will offer to their students innovative programmes backed by the appropriate resources to guarantee an excellent faculty body, an international experience and a multicultural environment.

The top business schools of the future will not only implement changes to remain competitive but they will seek accreditation and quality improvement programmes to prove to the market that they are committed to excellence and innovation.

But as business schools struggle to increase funding and spending to achieve greater value propositions, they will also need to adopt strategies that will allow them to differentiate themselves from their competitors and prove that value.

Quality will become an ever-growing concern for business schools, in particular with regard to measures for determining and improving the quality of programmes. The most competitive schools are already looking for benchmarking opportunities as well as quality improvement programmes that will provide them with an opportunity to gain a thorough understanding of their strengths and weaknesses, to develop new and better programmes, and to prove the level of their offerings to the market through accreditation. Students and faculty will also benefit greatly from having tools that aid them in their choice of institution and programme.

The link between the business and the academic worlds must also be strengthened and redesigned. It is clear that there is a need for a consultation process to discuss the definition of strategic objectives the development of shared infrastructures, and the production of competencies. This means that greater mutual understanding must be achieved, not just in general terms but also in specific areas such as recognition of the necessity of fundamental research and its connection to a productive economy.

I believe European governments need to offer strong incentives for a sufficiently long period so that a true culture of co-operation can be developed. Nor should we forget the individual at the heart of this mechanism - the teacher/researcher. It is urgent that incentives be established both to increase the percentage of young Europeans committed to following an academic career and also to ensure that they stay in Europe. It is urgent that remuneration levels be adjusted, either directly or indirectly, through the creation of an exceptional status akin to a "public safety" measure. This would partially compensate for the enormous amount of social status that this profession has lost.

I believe that we know what has to be done. Now we must show the courage and resilience to do it.

gf

Section_02
Business Models and the Paradigm Trap

"The market will be made by the leaders, by the forward-looking, innovative institutions that can test new programmes, attract students from around the world, and convince employers to recruit them"

Gordon Shenton and Patrice Houdayer
'The Bologna effect'

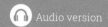 Audio version

Volume   Issue

01_02

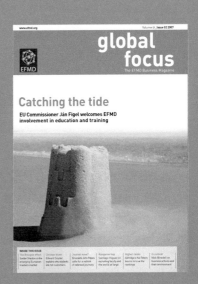

2007

The Bologna effect:
the emerging European masters market

GORDON SHENTON AND **PATRICE HOUDAYER** DESCRIBE HOW THE BOLOGNA PROCESS, ALONG WITH EUROPEAN-SPECIFIC ACCREDITATION AND RANKING SYSTEMS, IS REVOLUTIONISING THE EUROPEAN 'MARKET' IN MASTERS DEGREES AND GIVING IT GLOBAL COMPETITIVENESS

European business schools are in a much better position to compete in world education markets than was the case ten years ago. Beyond the qualitative improvement of many institutions individually, a number of factors of a systemic nature have contributed to this stronger competitive position.

The general background to this change has been the gradual emergence of a European market for management education that has impelled schools and universities to internationalise their activities beyond the borders of their home countries. This movement has itself occurred in a context in which a more structured world market has been steadily taking shape, reinforcing the need for European institutions to internationalise.

Three factors have accelerated this process of change.

First, rankings in the European press, notably in the *Financial Times,* have raised awareness within schools of their externally perceived positioning in international markets and encouraged them to improve their standing. European schools were used to the idea that, with a few exceptions such as London Business School, INSEAD and IMD, they carried little weight in American rankings and were mostly concerned about their position in their own national environment.

However, this all changed when the first serious and credible rankings began to appear in Europe itself. Not only were they able to see how they stood in comparison with American schools,

but they were confronted with their competitive standing on the European scene. "Being in the top 10 (or 15 or 25) in Europe" has become a popular strategic objective among business school deans as a first step towards establishing an international brand.

Second, the arrival of accreditation ten years ago, when the AACSB first began to assess schools internationally and when EQUIS was launched as an alternative, transformed the competitive environment in Europe. Business schools and university faculties of business and management have been driven to measure themselves against international standards of performance.

EQUIS in particular has turned a searchlight on a broad spectrum of quality criteria ranging across key areas such as effective governance, better qualified academic staff, improved programme quality, increased concern for the professional development and employability of students, stronger research capacity, and, of course, internationalisation.

The fact that Europe has been successful in establishing its own respected accreditation system has contributed to the global credibility of European management education. It is significant that, out of around 100 accredited schools and universities, close to one-third are from outside Europe, including leading institutions from around the world.

A third, decisive, factor in this strengthening of the international positioning of European business schools has been the impact of the Bologna reforms in higher education. Forty-five European countries have now committed

themselves to the creation of a more coherent European Higher Education Area with a target date of 2010 for completion of the structural reforms.

All the signatory countries have agreed to converge on a two-cycle system with a bachelors degree of not less than three years and a second masters level of an unspecified length, the objectives being to create "readable" degrees, to facilitate student mobility and to raise the competitiveness of European higher education on world markets.

Moreover, the bachelors degrees are intended to be a sufficient qualification for graduating students to enter directly into employment. This latter objective does, of course, raise very difficult problems in continental Europe where students are not used to leaving university after three years of study, where universities are used to keeping their students for five years and where employers are unaccustomed to recruiting students for managerial positions after three years of higher education.

EQUIS in particular has turned a searchlight on a broad spectrum of quality criteria ranging across a number of key areas

However, at the masters level, this clarification of degree formats and the introduction of internationally "readable" degree titles are proving to be significant marketing advantages, not only in Europe but on international markets generally. For the business schools and universities, these reforms have generalised for the whole of Europe an officially recognised masters market that previously only existed in a few countries, notably in Britain where the two-tier undergraduate/postgraduate, bachelors/masters organisation of higher education has been the norm. In continental Europe, the most common structure was formerly a four- or five-year curriculum leading to an advanced degree but with no significant intermediate degree after three years.

In the absence of any clear distinction between undergraduate and graduate levels, it was very difficult to argue that a degree obtained after five years of study was in reality the equivalent of a masters. As a result, these advanced degrees were often downgraded in international perception to the undergraduate level. In their negotiations with their American partners, for example, the French *grandes écoles* have struggled for decades to obtain graduate-level recognition for their five-year degrees.

This is not to say that there was no masters market in continental Europe before the Bologna reforms. Some institutions in, for example, France, Spain, Italy, the Netherlands and Scandinavia had been offering programmes carrying the masters label for many years, even though there was (at that time) no official government recognition of the degree. However, they were often private schools or spin-offs of a university business faculty operating outside the mainstream of higher education and dependent on market recognition.

It is in this context that the MBA has developed in continental Europe, independently of the public universities and outside the regulated degree systems. In this non-regulated environment, these schools have pioneered a uniquely European version of the MBA as a shorter, more focused, more corporate-oriented degree in which a concern for soft skills and personal development are paramount. However, the continental European masters market has remained small, underdeveloped in comparison with America or Britain and very uneven in its geographical spread from one country to another. Until very recently, for example, Germany was almost totally absent from the international MBA market.

Of course, a change of this magnitude is not occurring without a certain level of confusion. On the one hand, university faculties of business and management are faced with the difficult task of adjusting their educational mindset to the notion of a graduate curriculum that is other than simply the repackaging of the last one or two years of their previous five-year programmes.

A raft of thorny questions arises. How professionally oriented should these new masters programmes be? How specialised should they be? Should they be one-year or two-year programmes? Should it be a requirement to have studied at the bachelors level in the same field of study? Should admission to the masters level be automatic for a student who has completed the bachelors degree at the same university?

The risk is that in some cases change will be purely cosmetic, enough for formal compliance with the new laws but not sufficient to achieve the objectives set out in the Bologna agenda. Indeed, many universities are stuck in the middle of the change process, having made some accommodation to the new structure but without having given up many of the features of the old one. In these cases, the new degrees are even less "readable" than previously. One can charitably assume that these are growing pains and that the supply side of the market will eventually sort itself out. However, the essential point is that the opportunity now exists for the most innovative and progressive university-based institutions to seize market advantage in the new European arena.

> In the absence of any clear distinction between undergraduate and graduate levels, it was very difficult to argue that a degree obtained after five years of study was in reality the equivalent of a masters

10-25

Being in the top ten to 25 in Europe has become a popular strategic objective among business school deans as a first step towards establishing an international brand

Shenton:
new European arena

45

Forty-five European countries have now committed themselves to the creation of a more coherent European Higher Education Area

On the other hand, there is uncertainty as to how the new "Bologna" masters will co-exist with the previous postgraduate masters programmes that predate Bologna and that were designed from a different market perspective.

The position of the MBA, in particular, in the new emerging market is not entirely clear and there has been a risk that the MBA title would simply be used to describe the new Bologna pre-experience masters. Some difficulty also exists in repositioning the specialised postgraduate programmes that previously recruited students who had graduated with a first degree. In continental Europe, this meant recruiting students who had usually completed five years of higher education, up to a level that now corresponds to a masters.

Should institutions offering these degrees recruit at a lower age after a three-year bachelors programme? Or should they talk about an "advanced" masters and continue to recruit older students who already hold a masters degree?

These are issues that will be resolved in time as the market adjusts to the new situation. However, in parallel to the opening up of a masters market through the implementation of the Bologna agenda, an effort has been made within the management education community to clarify the nomenclature of masters degrees, given the extreme diversity within this category.

EFMD in collaboration with the EQUAL group of national associations has sought to distinguish between the MBA as a post-experience professional qualification and the new pre-experience generalist masters programmes which should carry another name such as a Masters in Management or MSc in Management. It is also recommending that the category of specialised Masters in Finance, Marketing, and so on should be distinguished both from the MBA, which is a generalist programme, and from the generalist Masters in Management for younger students. The aim has been not so much to regulate the market as to clarify the landscape so that students and the organisations that recruit them have an understanding of some basic distinctions.

These recommendations have been largely followed within the community of EQUIS accredited schools and beyond. A proof of this has been that the *Financial Times* now publishes an annual ranking of this new category of European Masters in Management, thus helping to raise awareness of the significance of this typically European qualification.

As a result of these convergent trends, a structured market for masters programmes in business and management is taking shape in Europe around three clearly differentiated segments: the MBA, which will now benefit from official recognition as a national degree in most countries; the generalist Masters in Management; and the specialised MSc programmes. The offering on this market is now much more understandable (or "readable" in the Bologna terminology) to all stakeholders both in Europe and in the rest of the world. Degree formats are now better aligned with the American and British systems and the use of the word masters to designate second-cycle degrees has put an end to the confusion caused by so many disparate names.

However, this offering is a specifically European one and is not simply a replica of the American market. The MBA, which has long been established in Europe, has evolved its own distinctive European characteristics. The Masters in Management, which is beginning to gain visibility, is also a characteristically European programme, different from the MBA, different from the four-year American undergraduate degree and different from the specialist MSc degrees. It is rooted in the European practice of pre-experience business education, combining at its best the academic rigour of the university tradition, practical exposure to the world of business and a highly developed international perspective. However, the particular mix and emphasis in each country will be different. Although the Masters in Management now has a transnationally recognisable format, it is not a standardised product since it reflects the diversity of culture, values and practice of more than 40 countries.

Thanks to the convergent impact of Bologna, of accreditation and of the rankings, European business schools and university faculties of business are potentially in a much stronger competitive position internationally. The emergence of a credible offering in all segments of the masters market should make it possible to increase inter-European student mobility and to attract increasing numbers of international students to European schools. In particular, the appearance of the Masters in Management as a globally recognisable product can for the first time draw mainstream European management education programmes into the world market.

How well and how extensively these opportunities are exploited will, of course, depend on the schools and universities themselves. The market is still unstructured, with many uncertainties regarding the behaviour of students and employers. There are legitimate doubts about the capacity of many European universities to transform their curricula and to make the necessary adjustments to their governance structures that would allow more market-oriented strategies. However, the market will be made by the leaders, by the forward-looking, innovative institutions that can test new programmes, attract students from around the world, and convince employers to recruit them.

Thanks to the convergent impact of Bologna, of accreditation and of the rankings, European business schools and university faculties of business are potentially in a much stronger competitive position internationally

ABOUT THE AUTHORS

Gordon Shenton is Associate Director of the EFMD's Quality Services Department and Emeritus Professor at EM-LYON Business School

Patrice Houdayer is Dean of Academic Programmes at EM-LYON Business School.

gf

Section_02
Business Models and the Paradigm Trap

"Strategic options, including part-time and on-line education, should encourage Deans and Directors of business schools to reflect genuinely on the long-term financial viability of their business models and focus on refreshing such models in the future"

Kai Peters and Howard Thomas
'A sustainable model for business schools?'

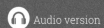 Audio version

Volume   Issue

05_02

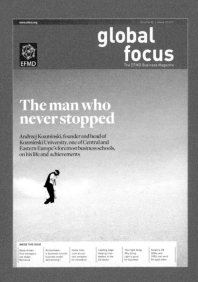

2011

A sustainable model for business schools?

Kai Peters and **Howard Thomas** argue that the current business model of business schools is financially unstable and probably unsustainable

At the core of each business school, a dialectic takes place between two distinct purposes – the goal of producing knowledge and the goal of educating students. Individual institutions have different views.

At one end of the spectrum there are research-intensive institutions while at the other there are teaching-led or even research-less schools. Most schools are somewhere in between, leaving them with a dual system of purposes and corresponding metrics that are all too often contradictory and confusing rather than cohesive.

The choices that individual institutions have made broadly share one common element. They are, the authors believe, financially unstable and probably unsustainable. This article therefore seeks to explore the financial drivers of business schools on both the income and expenditure sides of the equation and highlight areas of distinct concern for business school finances.

Where does the money come from?

£1k

In 1998 annual UK undergraduate fees of £1,000 were introduced...

£9k

... this will rise in 2012, in the majority of institutions, to £9,000

The state

Not all schools are dependent on government funding but many more are than are willing to admit. State funding means that schools are directly funded to educate students and additionally to produce research. Education is seen as a public good that produces an educated workforce, which in turn generates returns to the nation through higher productivity and taxes. Research generates innovation that also creates long-term public benefit.

While this traditional mode of funding is still strongly represented in continental Europe, it is increasingly being questioned on philosophical and financial grounds. In many nations, and especially in Asia and Latin America, education is viewed as largely a private rather than a public benefit and funding is being adjusted accordingly.

Whatever the merits of this debate, it is clear that it serves the purpose of governments to reduce education funding since they are facing intense competition for societal financial resources. Consequently, direct grants for education are being reduced and students are increasingly responsible for funding their own education.

Direct grants have thus become indirect grants via loans to students. In Britain this process has been underway for some time. While education was free for the user until 1997, fees have been increasing ever since.

In 1998 annual undergraduate fees of £1,000 were introduced. This increased to £3,000 in 2004 and will almost certainly rise to £9,000 at a majority of institutions in 2012.

At the same time as student debt increases, direct grants to universities for business education of approximately £3,500 per student will be removed in 2012. Graduates will be required to repay their loans over a lengthy period once they reach an annual income above £21,000.

The government is assuming that two-thirds of students will repay their loans. The university sector as a whole is expecting only one-third to repay. The truth will eventually become clear but perhaps not for as long as 30 years. Ironically, if eventual total repayments are less than 50% of the loans given out, the new system will be more expensive than the one it replaces.

Reliance on government is also the key driver where one would least expect to find it: in the American for-profit educational sector. The vast majority of students use federal loans to pay for their programmes.

For-profits are actually the largest users of federal funding. Without this funding, which is presently being challenged in Congress because of poor completion rates of between 10% and 15% of students in some cases, the business model of the for-profits will certainly be less attractive in the future.

Underlying these Anglo-American examples is the question of what proportion of a society ought to attend university. There are two different models for modern universities.

The Anglo-American model seeks broad participation. Approximately 50% of all secondary school graduates continue on to university. In the Humboldt university model, which is common in continental Europe, universities aim for a narrower intellectual elite in the range of 20% of high school graduates. In countries using the Humboldt model financing universities is less onerous.

In middle-income and developing countries, university attendance rates are more aligned with the Humboldt model, averaging, according to UNESCO, a UN agency, around 20%. The role of government funding is also more modest than in the west. Public funding accounts for 54% of university budgets whereas in OECD countries, approximately 76% of university funding originates from governments.

Student tuition

If the government is unwilling to pay, then the burden falls on the user of services. Undergraduate tuition fees are now beginning to rise steadily in many countries. Postgraduate fees, on the other hand, have for some time been largely free from constraints in terms of programme pricing and are seen as a key source of funding for many institutions.

The demand for postgraduate business education has increased dramatically over the last 20 years. Because of the imbalance between demand and supply, fees have increased rapidly. The cost of MBA tuition in Western Europe in the 1990s rarely surpassed €10,000; two decades later fees of €60,000 for full-time programmes are common, with some EMBAs now having price tags of over €100,000.

Tuition fees in America have reached extremely high levels. Presently, over 100 institutions charge over $50,000 a year for fees, room and board. On this basis and extrapolating from present trends, fees for four-year undergraduate degree programmes in America are likely to reach $330,000 by 2020. The top 20 MBA programmes in the US all ask tuition fees of around $100,000 while EMBA programmes cost up to $172,200.

Although historically students may have thought that the return on investment was not unreasonable, the increasing costs of tuition and living expenses combined with potential loss of income during the course may well lead to numerous candidates concluding that a tipping point will soon be reached where the costs outweigh the benefits.

Other sources of funding

Once government funding has decreased, business schools turn to two more sources of funding: executive education and fund raising. Both can be tremendously lucrative but are not necessarily easy to establish nor guaranteed to be successful. Executive education requires a different infrastructure and faculty composition than that of degree programmes.

Even when established, executive education is very volatile as illustrated by the impact of the current recession. Revenues reduced significantly within a matter of months. Unicon, a consortium of schools involved in executive education, reported that on average, revenues generated by executive education shrank by 30% in 2009 compared to 2008.

Fundraising is the other potentially large source of external funding and proud and satisfied alumni and friends of schools can be very generous. Certainly the endowments of the world's top ten universities are measured in billions rather than millions of euros.

However, expectations about amounts likely be generated by endowments have had to be amended recently as funds have shrunk in real terms as have returns. Furthermore, the number of universities where fundraising makes a substantial impact on operating budgets is actually very small.

||||||||||||||||||||||||||||||||||||||||||

€100k

The cost of MBA tuition in Western Europe in the 1990s rarely surpassed €10,000; two decades later fees of €60,000 for full-time programmes are common, with some EMBAs now having price tags of over €100,000

Where does the money go?

Academics – Research

In recent debates about higher education, one subject that has received only limited attention must surely be the model through which business schools and universities manage their main asset: their faculty.

In most academic institutions, overall staffing costs, including faculty, can easily approach 75% of institutional expenditures. These faculty members have priorities – teaching and research – that are often in conflict. In research-intensive universities as well as in many research-focused business schools, faculty members' career paths are dependent on their research productivity measured in the quality of research journals and the number of high-quality publications. Metrics are clear and are, unsurprisingly, output measures.

Input measures do not exist on the research front. How long does it take to write a paper? For some, a lifetime. For others, a weekend. Some individuals are able to develop collaborative infrastructures that include colleagues, graduate students and research assistants and as a result are able to generate many papers a year.

The point here is a simple one: how much time should be devoted to research in contrast to other activities? How much and what types of research output should be expected? Ultimately, can more time be freed up for other purposes such as teaching, managing or working with executives?

In some cases, research is directly funded or financed by research grants from foundations or directly from governments. But in most cases, research is cross-subsidised from teaching income. That is, premium-priced programmes such EMBAs become the "cash cows" for the funding of the school.

Academics – Teaching

The economics of teaching time is fascinating. The core question, surely, is what does an hour of teaching time cost, and what does an hour of teaching time generate as revenue? These core calculations can then be scaled up to an annual calculation and be compared across the higher educational landscape and with related, knowledge-intensive businesses.

At a base level, there are three research models in higher education. The first, a research-only model, will by necessity be left aside except as a cost to the institution that must be borne somehow.

The second is a teaching-intensive model. In many of the newer universities in Britain and elsewhere, there is an anchor at about 300 teaching hours a year. Assuming a base faculty salary of €50,000 with typical on-costs for pensions, support staff and so on, one can model a fully loaded cost of something in the region of €80,000 per faculty member. The teaching cost is thus about €270/hour.

At the research-intensive end of the spectrum, fully loaded salaries can be double. The main factor, however, is the reduced teaching load. At 120 teaching hours a year, the hourly teaching cost is about €1,350 though there are schools where average fully loaded salaries approach €250,000 with similarly low teaching loads. This leads to an hourly teaching cost of €2,200. No doubt someone somewhere is even more expensive on an hourly basis.

In comparison, secondary school teachers in middle income and developing economies cost, on average, €8/hour and in the OECD €34/hour.

Consulting firms have a similarly bullish approach to costs per hour. Given that consultants can easily have a target of generating 200 billable days, one will be looking at an hourly cost of something in the region of €45 for a mid-level consultant.

Given the economic infrastructure in place in higher education, there are two ways in which teaching costs can be managed.

The first is what seems to be the trend. Simply teach less. At undergraduate levels, contact time can appear rather thin with suggestions that six to ten contact hours per week for 30 weeks a year is not unusual. A second lever is simply to increase the number of students in the classroom to drive costs per students down.

Perhaps there is another option which needs to be considered. Is it realistic for universities to continue to operate with only their present range of models and levers or is it ultimately necessary to consider the unthinkable – increasing teaching loads across the sector?

Other

While overall staff proportions are actually quite stable across the higher education landscape, the proportion of academic to non-academic staff varies widely. Factors that have an impact include the product portfolio, the business school model, and in many cases the overall wealth and ambition of the institution. Marketing, for instance, will typically consume 8% to 12% of the MBA income stream.

||||||||||||||||||||||||||||||||||||||||||||||||||||

❝❞

Is it realistic for universities to continue to operate with only their present range of models and levers or is it ultimately necessary to consider increasing teaching loads across the sector?

Adding it all up

While not all business schools will face financial challenges in the near term, fault lines are clearly visible. Traditional sources of income are less stable. Government, the primary source of funding in the OECD countries, will not continue to expand educational budgets for ever. Examples to the contrary are already evident in many countries.

Student tuitions cannot go on rising forever. Many MBA programme fees, we believe, have reached levels that are not sustainable and raise a real question of value and fairness. Income from executive education or from donations can be substantial but is not in the reach of all schools.

On the cost side, we posit that many institutions are using a faculty model that is very luxurious. No other industries that we can think of use their main human capital to directly generate income for less than 10% of their annual time at one end of the spectrum or only about 30% at the other.

There are plenty of other challenges in the global market for education. These include the role of for-profits, the welcomed growth of middle income and developing world countries' own educational infrastructure, the advent of recessions and cost pressures in the competitive environment.

The consequent strategic options, including part-time and on-line education, should encourage Deans and Directors of business schools to reflect genuinely on the long-term financial viability of their business models and focus on refreshing such models in the future. **gf**

||||||||||||||||||||||||||||||||||||||||||||||||||||||||||||||||

ABOUT THE AUTHORS
Kai Peters is Chief Executive, Ashridge Business School.
||||||||||||||||||||||||||||||||||||||||||||||||||||||||||||||||

Howard Thomas is the Dean of Lee Kong Chian School of Business, Singapore Management University.
||||||||||||||||||||||||||||||||||||||||||||||||||||||||||||||||

Section_02
Business Models and the Paradigm Trap

"Whether we like it or not, business schools need to be managed in a business-like, professional and careful manner whether they are long-established incumbents or newcomers to business education or to one of the distinct value chains in the mix of programme possibilities"

Kai Peters, Howard Thomas and Rick Smith
'The Business of Business Schools'

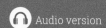 Audio version

Volume   Issue

12_01

gf

2017

Kai Peters, **Howard Thomas** and **Rick Smith** suggest that while much has been written about business schools from historical and critical perspectives not enough has emerged from an additional viewpoint – the lens of the business of business schools

The Business of Business Schools

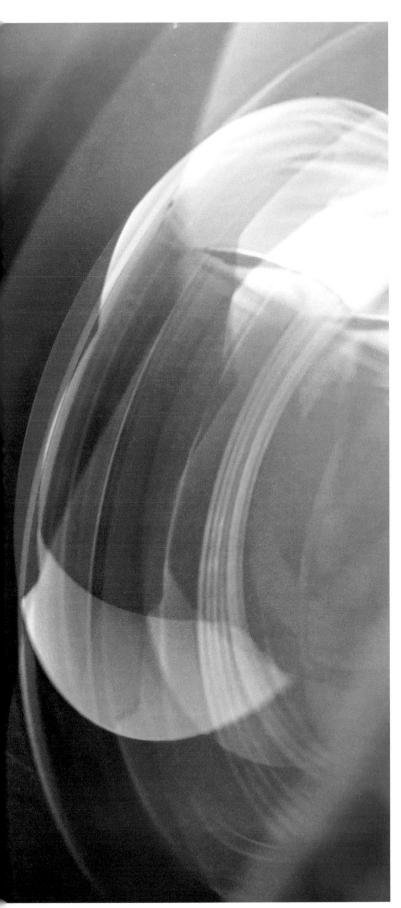

One can use any number of lenses to analyse the development of business schools over the past hundred or so years. But we now need an additional viewpoint – the lens of the business of business schools.

The historical lens

Rakesh Khurana, the renowned Harvard business school professor, has outlined the history and evolution of US business schools from their beginning in the late 19th and early 20th century. He shows how business schools evolved from, effectively, vocational trade schools through to their present state. He cites the tremendous influence that the Ford and Carnegie studies of 1959 had in the repositioning of business schools from practical institutions into academic behemoths.

These two studies, known as the Foundation Studies, are central to an understanding of business education and the business of business schools for every dean and senior business school manager around the world.

As Khurana outlines, foundations, between 1900 and 1935, provided 64% of all grants to US universities both for new initiatives and for existing institutions and thus their money has had tremendous influence over the direction of education.

After the second world war, both the Carnegie and Ford Foundations felt that business schools needed to professionalise and grow beyond their origins. Importantly, in the midst of the Cold War poor-quality business education was seen to threaten the health of the economy, democracy and the American way of life. By 1960, $35 million had been donated to a handful of business schools. And with that much money at stake, there were strings attached.

Schools were to professionalise, with faculty holding doctorates and producing graduate-level academic publications; students were to be taught quantitative methods and behavioural sciences – and only those academically qualified were to be admitted.

"

The "storm" of rankings changed everything. In simple terms and for better or worse, the advent of rankings in 1987 marked the dawn of the era of business schools as businesses with the rules of the game laid down by the Foundation Studies

And, while not obviously stated but clearly understood, schools were to have an anti-communist, pro-business and clearly capitalist orientation. While the grants that flowed in the 1950s set the scene, the 1959 Foundation Studies codified the expectations and created the framework for the dominant business school model and paradigm that still, for better or worse, exists today.

This paradigm also formed the basis for a second crucial driver in the business of business schools. In a 2005 article for AACSB's *BizEd*, Andy Policano, then Dean of UC Irvine in the US, wrote:

"Few people can remember what it was like before 1987 – what I call the year before the storm. It was a time when business school deans could actually focus on improving the quality of their schools' educational offerings. Discussions about strategic marketing were confined mostly to the marketing curriculum. PR firms were hired by businesses, not business schools. Most business schools had sufficient facilities, but few buildings had marble floors, soaring atriums, or plush carpeting. Public university tuition was affordable for most students, and even top MBA programs were accessible to students with high potential but low GMAT scores."

The "storm" of rankings changed everything. In simple terms and for better or worse, the advent of rankings in 1987 marked the dawn of the era of business schools as businesses with the rules of the game laid down by the Foundation Studies. Now, 30 years later, these rules of the game continue but have also evolved in the present era of disruption. As authors, our forthcoming book, *Disruption in Business Education*, Emerald Publishing 2017, investigates these challenges.

The Business Lens

As an organising principle in considering the management of the business school and the associated activities and offerings, consider a simple value chain. (See Figure 1.)

Not every school is active across the whole spectrum of programme possibilities and not all value chains will therefore carry the same relevance. Depending on the unique situation of each institution, the overall value chain will be re-configured to reflect the business system and processes of each level of a business school's offerings and activities

At each level, beginning with undergraduate education and proceeding along a probably arbitrary age-influenced continuum, there are different components that comprise that chain, drivers that are relevant, and the skills and competencies a school requires at that level. In sales and marketing terms, undergraduate education is a business-to-consumer and consumers-parent proposition with a path to market largely influenced by centralised placement services such as UCAS in the UK.

As one progresses along the age spectrum, the business-to-consumer model holds true for pre-experience postgraduate students but a centralised recruitment system no longer exists. For postgraduate, post-experience candidates, as for open-programme executive candidates, business-to-business consumer marketing is required and for executive education, business-to-business relationship marketing is needed.

Income varies considerably along this spectrum. For all of the business-to-consumer and business-to-business consumer programmes, income per day, what we phrase the "revenue-

€13k

The estimated number of business schools across the globe is over 13,000

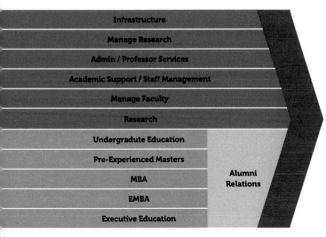

Infrastructure	
Manage Research	
Admin / Professor Services	
Academic Support / Staff Management	
Manage Faculty	
Research	
Undergradute Education	
Pre-Experienced Masters	Alumni
MBA	Relations
EMBA	
Executive Education	

Figure 1

€2k

Custom organisation
development consulting
can generate only
€2,000 per faculty day

€200k

The US EMBA programmes
can generate €200,000
per faculty day. Between
undergraduate and
postgraduate programmes,
revenue can easily vary
between €2,000 per day
and €30,000 per day

delivered-view" is a straight-forward calculation of tuition x classroom occupancy / days taught.

For customised executive education and similar business to business activities, a comparable calculation sometimes holds true.

More often than not, however, day rates are contractually fixed and are not a direct factor of participant numbers. The variance in income is tremendous. Where custom organisation development consulting can generate only €2,000 per faculty day, the pricey US EMBA programmes can generate €200,000 per faculty day. Between undergraduate and postgraduate programmes, revenue can easily vary between €2,000 per day and €30,000 per day.

While we do not propose running business schools purely on the basis of income per day, surely knowing income per day could aid in sensible decision making. Alas, we do not see many schools calculate along these lines.

Beyond income levels per activity, equally important to examine are the increasing elements of disruption and substitution that have come to play a significant role in the business school landscape.

Schools increasingly face "make or buy" decisions at practically each stage of the value chain. At one end of the spectrum there are schools where almost everything is managed and delivered in-house. At the other end, there are schools that function largely as co-ordinating mechanisms for the purchasing of external services. At nearly every stage of the continuum there are now complementary service providers who will come to the aid of schools to help them provide needed capabilities.

Figure 2

Figure 2 diagram labels:

Support Activities:
- Infrastructure
- Manage Research
- Admin / Professor Services
- Academic Support / Staff Management
- Manage Faculty
- Research

Value Creation:
- Undergradute Education
- Pre-Experienced Masters
- MBA
- EMBA
- Executive Education

Alumni Relations

Undergradute Education — Find Students — House and Feed Students — Teach Students — Give Students Space and Technology — Graduate Students — Place Students

The undergraduate value chain illustrated in Figure 2 is an example of the various stages in the educational process. "Finding students" has become an industry in itself. Nearly 40% of international students are recruited via agents overall, with about 55% of students in Australia and 11% of students in the US forming the "bookends".

While many agents are small operations, increasing numbers of large players have emerged who recruit, often house and sometimes teach foundation degrees and pre-sessional English to students. While most business schools supplement core teaching capacity with adjuncts and associates for special skills and flexibility, a school can, and many do, use only adjuncts to teach. In the past year, we have become aware of specialist agencies who supply a roster of teaching capacity to a number of London-based branch campuses of regional UK universities.

Providing students with technology or, better said, providing white-label online education is also a big business. Business schools can source provision in exchange for income-sharing arrangements with a significant number of potential partners who will build single programmes or a whole range of programmes, including MOOCs.

Finally, to round things off, business schools can be set up and run using degree-awarding powers from another educational provider. At the moment, there are over 700,000 students studying for UK degrees outside the UK. This is more than the number of students actually studying at degree-awarding institutions inside the UK.

The services, noted above, do not come cheap nor minus attached strings. Getting it wrong, allowing external providers to cherry-pick lucrative services and price them to their own advantage rather than to the advantage of a school is something we have seen increasingly over the past decade.

While agency relationships tend to be multiple and local, student housing or online relationships tend to be large and long-term. Business schools increasingly find large multi-national players with comprehensive legal departments and sophisticated contracting on the other side of the negotiating table. Business schools, on the other hand, tend to be well-meaning amateurs and SMEs in comparison.

Whether we like it or not, business schools need to be managed in a business-like, professional and careful manner whether they are long-established incumbents or newcomers

700k

At the moment, there are over 700,000 students studying for UK degrees outside the UK. This is more than the number of students actually studying at degree-awarding institutions inside the UK

Whether we like it or not, business schools need to be managed in a business-like, professional and careful manner whether they are long-established incumbents or newcomers to business education or to one of the distinct value chains in the mix of programme possibilities

to business education or to one of the distinct value chains in the mix of programme possibilities.

If this short article or our longer book achieves one thing it will be to encourage business schools to think through the consequences, short-term and long-term, of their own structures and financial arrangements.

Adapted from: *Rethinking the Business Models of Business Schools: A Critical Review and Change Agenda,* Emerald Publishing January 2018. Kai Peters, Richard R. Smith, and Howard Thomas.

ABOUT THE AUTHORS

Kai Peters is Pro-Vice-Chancellor of Business & Law, Coventry University, Coventry, UK.

Richard R Smith is Professor of Strategic Management (Practice), Lee Kong Chian School of Business, Singapore Management University, Singapore and Associate Dean of the business school at SMU.

Howard Thomas is LKCSB Distinguished Term Professor of Strategic Management and Management Education, Lee Kong Chian School of Business, Singapore Management University, Singapore.

Section_02
Business Models and the Paradigm Trap

"Research is one of the most valuable assets of the academic world, and should be encouraged and increased. Sadly, at times of crisis, research, development and innovation spending tends to be the first to be axed, a policy that in the long term leads only to loss of competitiveness and innovative capacity"

Santiago Iñiguez
'Needed: academic Triathletes'

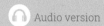 Audio version

Volume   Issue

06_02

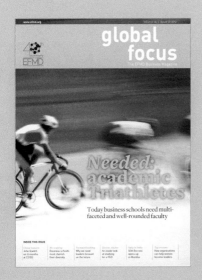

2012

" Today's academics might usefully
be compared to the classical athletes,
insomuch as they must show excellence
in a number of fields – research, teaching
and involvement in the world of business

Needed:
academic
Triathletes

Santiago Iñiguez argues that what business schools
need today is multi-faceted and well-rounded faculty

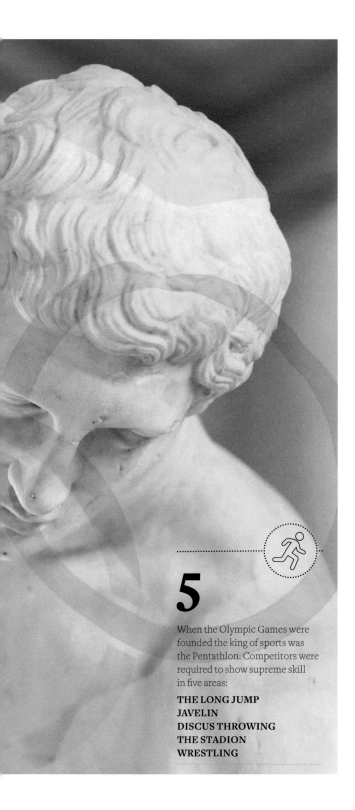

5

When the Olympic Games were
founded the king of sports was
the Pentathlon. Competitors were
required to show supreme skill
in five areas:

**THE LONG JUMP
JAVELIN
DISCUS THROWING
THE STADION
WRESTLING**

When the Olympic Games were founded in Ancient Greece sometime during the eighth century BC, the king of sports was the Pentathlon. As its name suggests, competitors were required to show supreme skill in five areas: the long jump; javelin; discus throwing; the *stadion* (or 180-meter race); and wrestling.

Nobody is sure how the winner of the Pentathlon was established, perhaps by winning three events and doing well in two others. Whatever the method, whenever the Olympics came along, the winners of the Pentathlon were the new heroes. Aristotle, in his *Rhetoric*, tells us that the participants in this sport were the most complete athletes and were honoured with medals and commemorative urns.

When it was decided to revive the Olympic Games at the end of the 19th century, other combined sports were devised, aimed at measuring the overall athletic ability of participants and favouring in many ways the traditional amateur spirit of the Games. Contestants were not professional athletes nor were they usually specialists in a particular sport. Some of these multi-events have survived to this day, notably the Triathlon, made up of swimming, cycling, and running.

Translated to the world of business education, today's academics might usefully be compared to the classical athletes, insomuch as they must show excellence in a number of fields. The academic race is essentially a Triathlon, made up of three main activities: research, teaching and involvement in the world of business – sometimes through consulting or by holding a management or board post.

However, success as an academic has traditionally been tantamount to excellence in research, period. Universities have conventionally selected, promoted, tenured and rewarded scholars who comply with certain requirements related to research activity and output.

Other facets of academic life such as teaching, the spreading of knowledge or interacting with the world outside universities have been considered as secondary activities for an academic career, sometimes even as "improper".

Nobody could reasonably deny the central value that research should play in scholarly careers. It is probably the core activity of the Academic Triathlon since it tests the capacity of the individual to assimilate existing knowledge and to generate new ideas, concepts and models, and at the same time respecting methodological rigor.

However, considering research as an end in itself or the only pure academic activity entails a myopic and incomplete version of the academic vocation.

Revealingly, an article in the *New York Times* described how a Harvard team formed by nine prominent professors of the university and supported by its former President, Derek Bok, was leading an effort to foster the culture of undergraduate teaching and learning.

"The group has issued a report calling for sweeping institutional change, including continuing evaluation and assessment of teaching and learning, and a proposal that teaching be weighed equally with contributions to research in annual salary adjustments." (S Rimer, 'Harvard Task Force Calls for New Focus on Teaching and Not Just Research', *The New York Times*, May 10, 2007.

The need to complement research with teaching and practical work is particularly relevant for business school academics.

Management education requires a special sort of scholar, professionals who can combine many different facets, from a solid research background to the ability to perform effectively in class and to interface with top managers.

I have often said that business schools need not only "Gurus" – wise sages who originate new thought but also "Kangurus" – academics able to jump from their research tasks to teaching and from there to consultancy or an interview with a journalist.

Kangurus of this type are not born but trained and it normally requires a wide career span to exploit the necessary synergies between those different, apparently contradictory but actually intertwined activities.

One of the main missions of business schools is to build bridges between academia and companies, between the world of thinking and research and the practical world of business.

Academic research makes a vital contribution to our body of knowledge on management. Research methodologies bring the rigor and objectivity required for a clear analysis of reality and allow us to come up with solutions based on comparative studies.

In fact, I believe that much of the blame for the recent financial crisis could be attributed to models and ideas from institutions that lacked the rigor that is a feature of academic research.

The reputation of a business school is directly related to the research and knowledge that it produces. From my experience with our stakeholders, and particularly with corporate universities, a key criterion in choosing a school to provide customised programmes is its capacity for generating new knowledge.

> **" "** *I believe that much of the blame for the recent financial crisis could be attributed to models and ideas from institutions that lacked the rigor that is a feature of academic research*

In his book (*Thought Leadership Meets Business: How Business Schools Can Become More Succesful* (Cambridge: Cambridge University Press, 2008, p. 182), Peter Lorange also highlighted the need for business schools to adopt an "interactive, two-way approach, where propositional knowledge meets prescriptive knowledge". This mutually beneficial virtuous cycle can be seen in executive education or MBA programmes where participants have considerable experience, giving teachers the opportunity to benefit from feedback by professionals attending their classes.

Despite constant criticism to the opposite, business schools are in reality proactive when it comes to developing the mechanisms needed to change the systems that generate and distribute knowledge.

This is shown by a concern for strengthening the clinical relevance of research, reflected in the significant number of articles on the subject published in recent years by the Academy of Management, the most influential forum on a global level for academic research into management.

To return to the analogy with Ancient Greece, below are some further proposals that might contribute to strengthening the links between Academia and the *Agora* (the market).

Redesign PhD management programmes so that participants, aside from developing the skills of sound researchers, are also given the opportunity to practise the complementary facets that will allow them to teach effectively and also to take advantage of teaching to disseminate the results of their own research.

What's more, doctoral programmes should also facilitate contact between students and business leaders to give them first-hand experience of the real problems of management. This could also be achieved through internships.

Adapt tenure systems to take into account not only candidates' published academic output but also their teaching skills. Furthermore, it would be advisable to introduce procedures to evaluate to what extent teachers maintain links with the world of business, either through membership of boards or consulting work. Obviously, overall

The head of a corporate university told me recently that companies are attracted mainly by business schools associated with new ideas and innovation.

To make business schools' research more relevant, I believe that it is necessary to come up with constructive proposals that will strengthen the ties between the academic and business worlds.

In line with the arguments of Costas Markides, a professor at London Business School, who calls for "ambidextrous professors", I think that it is a mistake to underestimate both the value of academic research or of integrative analysis. To do so will lead to the disappearance of a highly valuable and essential approach that has provided rigor to the management knowledge base we currently draw on.

I also agree with Professor Markides that it is a mistake to foster the separation between research academics and practitioners. (See his article "In Search of Ambidextrous Professors", *Academy of Management Journal* Vol. 50, No. 4 (2007), 762-768.)

His proposals to encourage younger scholars to publish not just in academic journals but also in professional publications are the way forward.

In this way we will see the transfer of research into teaching as well as encouraging co-operation between businesses and consultancies to identify new ideas and models for research.

evaluation will still emphasise research output; the challenge is to find a balance that will allow teachers to incorporate these proposals over time. Once again, the Triathlon analogy comes to mind.

The proposals mentioned above would probably require evaluation periods of at least one year to provide sufficient perspective on the results and impact in each of the areas.

Work with business leaders to identify the key issues affecting the business world. A growing number of business schools have already set up interdisciplinary centres aimed at going beyond the remit of traditional academic departments by setting up direct links with companies to develop specific projects. These centres not only encourage interdisciplinary research but also develop training programmes that address specific issues relating to business management.

At the same time, it is important that business schools' boards and advisory councils understand the strengths and weaknesses of their respective institutions. These councils are generally made up of business people or alumni who can provide invaluable feedback on what the real world's knowledge needs are.

Encourage ties between research-oriented teachers and practitioners. So far, this kind of co-operation has usually been restricted to developing teaching material for programmes. But it can be extended to other areas. Responsibility for bringing together the two should be a key objective of department heads, who can advance joint research initiatives.

Develop procedures to assimilate knowledge produced outside the academic environment. Business schools should act as knowledge hubs, bringing in new ideas, concepts and models generated outside their immediate sphere, for example in consultancies, corporate universities and other forums. New communication and information technologies offer limitless potential for testing and developing ideas.

Appoint "embedded academics" within companies. This would be another step toward setting up chairs financed by companies in business schools. The professors appointed to these chairs would work on specific projects with the sponsoring companies. This approach is already in use among consultancies,

which send consultants into a company for long-term or highly important projects. "Embedded academics" would have one foot in academia and another in the business world.

At IE business school in Madrid, Spain, we have already put this approach into practice: we have a Human Resources Chair sponsored by leading Spanish fashion retailer group Inditex and Accenture's Competitive Strategy Chair. The professors who hold the chairs spend a significant amount of their time working on specific projects with the companies involved, at the same time pursuing relevant and up-to-the-minute academic research in their respective areas.

Develop ways to measure the impact of academic research on the real world. This would mean going beyond the standard bibliometric indicators or article citation rates. We know that in management, as in the social sciences, the impact of ideas cannot just be measured by how often they are turned into patents or registered as inventions, the approach generally used in other scientific disciplines.

I would suggest two approaches:

• recognising a piece of academic work on the basis of its inclusion in management programmes taught around the world; for example, models or concepts such as the Balanced Scorecard, Blue Ocean Strategies or Non-market Strategies, which are now part of just about every MBA programme

• bringing together academics from business schools, corporate universities, development departments, consultancies and even the publishers of management publications to design systems that would allow for periodic analysis of research produced by schools and their use as management tools in the business world. Ideally, this would come up with a range of measuring systems reflecting diverse cultural and business practices and thus the heterogeneity of the research.

Research is one of the most valuable assets of the academic world, and should be encouraged and increased. Sadly, at times of crisis, research, development and innovation (R+D+I) spending tends to be the first to be axed, a policy that in the long term leads only to loss of competitiveness and innovative capacity.

It is essential to raise awareness of the value of academic research for the business world, and this is something in which business schools can play a key role. **gf**

ABOUT THE AUTHOR

Santiago Iñiguez is the Dean of IE Business School, Madrid, Spain

This is an adapted and edited extract from Santiago Iñiguez's book *The Learning Curve: How Business Schools Are Reinventing Education* (London: Palgrave Macmillan 2011)

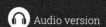
Section_02
Business Models and the Paradigm Trap

"The demands placed on universities have grown over the last few years, not only with regard to research, teaching and other related demands (now often known as 'third mission activities') but also in connection with universities' role as employers"

Edeltraud Hanappi-Egger
'Assessing academics' performance'

🎧 Audio version

Volume   Issue

11_02

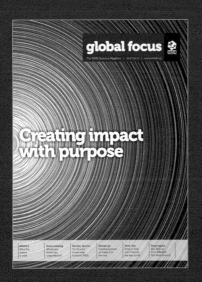

2017

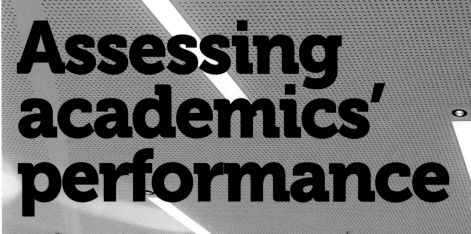

Assessing academics' performance

Is it time for a change in faculty recruitment and promotion practices? **Edeltraud Hanappi-Egger** describes how, and why, business schools need to take into account multiple aspects of performance

Masters degree – PhD – postdoc – assistant professor – full professor.

That's what most people expect an academic career to look like – a linear, full-time post in academia from a degree programme to a tenured professorship at a renowned university of business and economics.

A career like this often implies that academics are expected to churn out publication after publication. But when it comes to recruiting researchers for senior faculty positions or to promoting academics, it is not enough to focus mainly on the number of publications in top-tier journals; various other aspects play a crucial role in the performance portfolio of academics.

This is especially true because the demands placed on universities have grown over the last few years, not only with regard to research, teaching and other related demands (now often known as "third mission activities") but also in connection with universities' role as employers.

What do we mean by performance?

WU (Vienna University of Economics and Business) is breaking new ground in this area and has been discussing a more comprehensive in-house performance assessment system for full professors. In addition, the diversity of researchers' personal contexts has been taken into account in various guidelines for evaluating the performance of faculty members.

The current discussion on how to measure multiple aspects of performance at WU is inspired by the approach of measuring achievement or performance relative to opportunity, which is primarily used by universities in Australia and New Zealand.

At the core of this approach lies the concept that the traditional model of a full-time, linear, uninterrupted academic career can no longer be taken as the norm and the main yardstick for measuring performance.

WU hopes to initiate a process that allows us to rethink the way performance is assessed in academia, both at WU itself and also at other universities.

uLiKe, WU's multi-dimensional in-house performance assessment system, is intended to include diverse criteria that go beyond publication output and give more weight to teaching, knowledge transfer activities and/or work in university development

The goal is to develop a new, more comprehensive understanding of performance and performance assessment methods in the academic field, focusing on the quality, impact and consistency of researchers' achievements while also taking into account specific personal contexts. With this new approach, WU aims to contribute to a discussion on performance assessment procedures at universities.

Is it still enough to measure performance based on research output alone?

Which criteria should be applied to judge performance? A look at international rankings and rating systems shows that the performance of researchers is usually assessed based on research output, which, in turn, is mainly gauged quantitatively using criteria such as publication counts and impact factors.

But though this approach is widely regarded as neutral and objective, it has some pitfalls. In particular, the conventional performance assessment system gives an advantage to those researchers who work in well-established fields with a long tradition of publication and who pursue publication strategies that emphasise quantity.

However, these systems do not give adequate recognition to academic achievements in innovative fields that do not have a long tradition of publication opportunities.

Performance measurements focusing mostly on research output also fail to reward important work in teaching and third mission activities.

If universities place paramount importance on publication output, early-career scholars have to work very hard to meet these specific performance standards. This puts pressure on researchers to follow a strict lifestyle that allows them to dedicate themselves fully to research and to work with a tight focus on goals, independence and undivided attention. As a consequence, a standard career path with uninterrupted, linear full-time employment remains a common requirement for being able to perform adequately.

Since career paths have changed significantly over recent years, there are more and more researchers who for a variety of reasons might complete their PhD at age 35 instead of 25 maybe because they had a job during their studies, started their degree programme late or – for whatever reason – took some time off.

Women, particularly, can find it very hard to meet the demands of academia because their academic portfolios and career paths are often "non-standard".

For these reasons, it is probably a good idea to assess a researcher's publication output relative to his or her so-called "academic age" – the time passed since completion of the PhD, regardless of actual age. This means that performance measurements will give a better picture of an individual's capabilities if their life stories and the opportunities they have had are taken into account.

Multi-dimensional performance assessment in academia

In addition to the biographical contexts of academics, it also seems to be necessary to broaden performance assessment approaches by including more factors than just research output understood in terms of publication count.

uLiKe, WU's multi-dimensional in-house performance assessment system, is intended to include diverse criteria that go beyond publication output and give more weight to teaching, knowledge transfer activities and/or work in university development. In concrete terms, this means that performance in the area of research is evaluated based on criteria such as the number of original articles, original contributions to journals and books, or third-party funding that is attracted.

At the same time, however, the new approach also looks at achievements in the field of teaching, factoring-in aspects such as courses taught, thesis supervision, assistance provided to early-stage researchers and student ratings.

Third mission activities are also becoming more and more important for universities. For this reason, additional factors should be considered, including work in university management or decision-making bodies, committee membership, work as a reviewer or assessor, active co-operation with partner universities as well as work for the academic community, for example, functions performed for academic societies or journals (work as an editorial board member or reviewer) or contributing to the organisation of conferences.

Third mission activities relevant to performance assessment also include services to society and knowledge transfer, including offering academic expertise to the media, writing popular science articles and giving presentations at non-academic events.

It is important to note that all professors should be involved in third mission work in one way or another.

All these activities could be assessed relative to individual personal contexts. Relevant factors include caring for children or family members, leaves of absence, part-time employment and gaps in academic career paths due to illness or involvement in civil society initiatives.

In some areas, WU has made previous efforts to acknowledge the importance of a comprehensive range of criteria in assessing employee performance. In 2013, for example, a WU working group developed a definition of the job profile of a full professor that bases performance assessment on an extended range of qualification criteria in the fields of research, teaching and third mission activities.

To take into account personal aspects in assessing applicants for a position as a full professor, WU drew up an information document for search committees and guidelines for reviewers in senior faculty recruitment, in accordance with the provisions of WU's Plan for the Advancement of Women.

In addition, a special assessment sheet is available to search committee members and reviewers to help them understand and apply the position announcement criteria and to improve transparency. A note has also been added to the catalogue of questions for employee performance reviews as a reminder that an employee's publication output should be assessed in the

context of his or her biography, taking into consideration, for example, part time arrangements.

Position announcements for full professorships also contain an explicit note that applicants are expected to have an excellent research output relative to their "academic age". This means that performance is seen in relation to a person's individual context.

These new announcements send out important signals to society. They encourage young researchers to apply because they know that their research output will be assessed relative to their academic age and other work and responsibilities. This approach is intended to broaden the palette of criteria applied when reviewing candidates' qualifications. Of course, all these measures by no means imply that we plan to expect less from our applicants.

Further steps towards equal opportunities

There have many been efforts in academia to make performance assessment more transparent and to eliminate certain discriminatory effects of common performance evaluation methods. At some Austrian universities, special workshops are held to raise awareness of these issues. Other approaches seek to improve transparency and equal opportunities by limiting the number of publications considered, for example by basing the evaluation of candidates on a limited number of each applicant's best publications.

As a next step, these approaches should be combined and refined into a multi-dimensional system that can then be translated into various guiding principles. The goal is to make further steps towards equal opportunities for researchers with non-standard biographies who show excellent performance in activities that go beyond just research output.

The goal is to make further steps towards equal opportunities for researchers with non-standard biographies who show excellent performance in activities that go beyond just research output

'How many papers is a baby worth'

It goes without saying that the transition towards a more comprehensive performance assessment framework that includes personal contexts also creates certain challenges.

It requires intensive dialogue and discussion on the selection of criteria and personal factors to be included in performance assessment and how these factors should be weighted. This is by no means a trivial process because it is hard to measure how many papers should be seen as equivalent to child care or caring obligations, for example. (See Klocker N, Drozdzweski D. (2012): *Career progress relative to opportunity: How many papers is a baby "worth"?* Environment and Planning A 44, p. 1271-1277.)

Another issue is that specific biographical factors can only be taken into consideration if they are disclosed. But how can people be encouraged to share private information for the purpose of performance assessment? Disclosing such information obviously blurs the borders between private and work life, which may be seen as problematic by some and is an issue that needs to be addressed.

It is also essential to discuss how we can make sure that the new approach to more comprehensive performance assessment does not lead to a drop in quality standards and that it is not used to justify sub-par performance.

Indeed, the opposite may even be the case with the addition of new performance assessment criteria making it harder rather than easier for people with non-standard biographies to meet all the different demands. After all, would the requirement to engage in third mission knowledge transfer and supervise theses on top of conventional research work pose an additional burden for researchers with child care obligations?

A stimulus for further development

The question of how a more comprehensive performance assessment system can be implemented and put into practice must undoubtedly be answered by each university individually, and the process requires a great deal of discipline and commitment on the part of the entire faculty.

We believe, however, that initiating this process of change is well worth the effort, as is evidenced by the Diversitas award WU received from the Austrian Federal Ministry of Science, Research and Economy in December 2016.

WU has since been approached by several universities that are interested in the project. Ample positive feedback and strong interest from the media are further signs that it is high time to start a large-scale process of change that involves multiple universities.

Please do not hesitate to contact me for further information.

gf

ABOUT THE AUTHOR
Professor Edeltraud Hanappi-Egger is Rector of WU (Vienna University of Economics and Business) and Vice-President of Universities Austria (uniko). She is Professor of Gender and Diversity in Organisations.

Section_03
Rigour-Relevance and Business School Impact

"Co-production depends on relationships. You can't do it if you don't get out beyond the boundaries of the university and meet people, engage with them, talk to them and develop good personal relationships. To me it's fundamentally about relationship building and a willingness to experiment"

Andrew Pettigrew
'Scholarly impact and the co-production hypothesis'

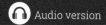 Audio version

Volume   Issue

02_02

gf

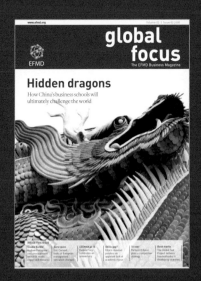

2008

How can we make academic research into management more
relevant to practitioners? **Andrew Pettigrew** has some suggestions.

'Scholarly impact' and the co-production hypothesis

There is, to say the least, some scepticism throughout the management community about the impact of management research – who listens, who notices, what consequences does it have? This is something that scholars and also potential users of management research are increasingly concerned about.

There are a number of hypotheses one can make about how this situation can be improved; how research into management issues can be both of a high scholarly quality and of real use to practitioners. In other words, how do we give management research "scholarly impact"?

The first hypothesis is that scholars in the area should have the aspiration to do both scholarly and practical research work – to tackle the "double hurdle".

The second concerns the quality of relationships held by the academics and the ability sometimes to work through "knowledge brokers", or intermediaries.

Third is the quality of ideas.

Finally, the key hypothesis concerns the co-production of research by scholars and practitioners.

The 'double hurdle'

Research into management often seems to be a dichotomy – you either have an impact on scholarship or you have an impact on the worlds of policy and practice. But rather, we should aspire to meet a double hurdle, where we seek to do work that has both a quality of scholarship and a practical impact.

The current reality of course is that people diverge and define themselves either as a scholar, spending all their time writing articles and books and others who define themselves as an applied researcher or consultant and don't worry too much about where their work is published but much more concerned about who they can influence in the "real" world.

It's rare to find people who aspire to produce work of the highest scholarly quality and deal with practical issues at the same time. Our aim should be to encourage people to aspire to this.

It will involve a cultural change that will shift people's focus from publishing output, writing articles and books – which to me is an intermediate good – to the final good, which is having scholarly and practical impact. At lot of the incentive systems in academia have unwittingly focused people on the intermediate good.

This is not to decry the value of published research but somehow we have to turn people's gaze from this intermediate good to the final good. And that will not be easy.

Relationships

Another issue is the problem of engaging with potential users of research. The one thing we know about user engagement is that very often it depends on how particular issues are regarded at the time by potential users – are these issues rising or falling in their list of priorities?

Often, too, they become interested in something because they know, or have heard of, the academic involved. It's really about brands. For example, Michael Porter is a "brand" and

IMAGES COURTESY: SCHOOL OF MANAGEMENT, UNIVERSITY OF BATH

therefore what he says is likely to generate interest and to be accepted as authentic. The same is true of certain research centres and other institutions that have gained general public acclaim. The Centre for Economic Performance at the London School of Economics, for example, can be characterised as such a brand, as can the respected Institute for Fiscal Studies, also in the UK.

And it is because they are so influenced by branding, by the reputation of individual academics or of the centres where they work, that potential users of research can be fickle.

If the director of an institution changes, something goes with him or her. Some users may walk away because their allegiance was to that person.

So user receptivity is unpredictable and person-dependent. It's built on relationships.

It's also dependent on context and timing.

As an academic you can come forward with some really great concept or idea – let's say it's about technological change and find that there's absolutely no interest in it whatsoever. Three years later something has stirred up the political nest and everybody is fixated with technological change.

This means that academics have to be visible over the long term. They have to have sustainable long-term relationships.

What I think this means for younger scholars is that they not only have to develop intellectual capital as they build up their work they also have to develop social capital.

Some of them may know that intuitively but my feeling is that they don't go out and deliberately build networks.

But if you want your work to have impact then you must be a networker. You've not only got to have relationships but you also have to know how to sustain them and how to exploit them.

And these networks must be global. One of the problems I see at the moment is that too many European academics are becoming rather self-concerned with their own academic institutions. This is fine. But if it is at the expense of neglecting North American institutions then it is a mistake. Networks must be global and building networks in North America is particularly important to this.

> It is because potential users of research are so influenced by branding, by the reputation of individual academics or of the centres where they work, that they are so fickle

These networks should also extend to the corporate world. If you are an expert in, say, the financial services industry you need to know chief executives, senior people, strategy people in the big banks.

It also means having networks inside government, knowing senior civil servants, consulting firms, think tanks, even journalists, who often act as translators and amplifiers of academic work in the management field. The fact that someone writes about your work in the *Financial Times* make people interested.

The quality of ideas

Another issue is the belief that some people have is that dissemination is impact – "if only I could write better or talk like Tony Blair, then there wouldn't be a problem. We are such dreadful communicators but if only I could disseminate better then there wouldn't be a problem".

To me that is fantasy and trivialises the problem. I'm not denying the importance of dissemination or skill in writing or talking because we are in the influence business and people influence through the written and spoken word. But no matter how good a communicator you are, if you ask the wrong questions and pose them in the wrong areas then no amount of accessible or skilful communication will produce any sort of impact.

Dissemination is not impact. You can't guarantee impact just by writing well or talking well. You have to ask the right questions, pursue the right themes at the right time. Accessibility on its own is not enough. There is a dissemination issue but not just a dissemination issue.

Co-production

This leads on to the key hypothesis of co-production.

I can sit here and work on my own or with other academics and that's fine. But if I go out and say I want to work with McKinsey or PwC or whoever on this, that doesn't mean setting up an advisory group so that they come here and give me advice.

Co-production means the involvement of partners throughout the complete cycle of research. First, it involves the scoping and direction of a research project; second, the commissioning of research; third, the leading and managing of research; and fourth, the delivering of the research results and ensuring their impact.

The hypothesis here is that early and continuous engagement increase the probability of impact. There is no set model for co-production and it is encouraging that many scholars are now willing to experiment with various forms of engagement to see which works most effectively.

Of course, the complete antithesis to co-production is what one might call "smash and grab" research, which, amazingly enough, is still going on. Smash and grab research involves a highly unilateral state of affairs where a scholar can gain access

No matter how good a communicator you are, if you ask the wrong questions and pose them in the wrong areas then no amount of accessible or skilful communication will produce any sort of impact

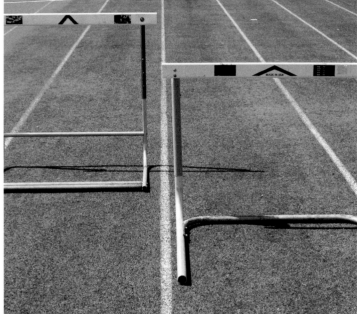

to an organisation, go and grab the information and data, and then write it all up in scholarly isolation.

Not only is this unfair to the organisation it is also unfair to other scholars who may come along later and be refused access to the same organisation because of the poor behaviour of their predecessors.

Again, my hypothesis is that co-production, this involvement in the whole research cycle from the inception to the dissemination, increases the probability of impact. You can't guarantee it, of course, but you increase the probability of impact. And I want people to experiment in this co-production of knowledge.

Co-production depends on relationships. You can't do it if you don't get out beyond the boundaries of the university and meet people, engage with them, talk to them and develop good personal relationships so that they say "well I don't mind working with this guy, it sounds OK, we might get something good out of it". To me it's fundamentally about relationships building and also about a willingness to experiment.

The corporate world is much more open to this kind of thing than you might imagine. But again it's often very person-specific. You can go to x number of people in a big company and most will be indifferent but you will find some people who see the value in it.

They see the value because they are going to learn from direct engagement with the scholar and be capturing the findings earlier, not waiting to read a great academic tome three years down the track. If you're working as a team then you are capturing the value as the value is being created rather than waiting for it to materialise.

Other things you can do if you are engaged like this is to help shape the project – and that increases the commitment of the person to the process. And they are also much more likely to co-fund if they co-produce. Now of course this has been going on for years in areas such as engineering; it's nothing new, it's not some great invention.

Of course, this may be seen by some academic as very close to a form of consulting, as not "pure" research but "getting into bed with the devil" and becoming an applied researcher.

But it need not be. Academics can fashion and shape the work so that all the interests of the various parties are met without compromising the important academic values of independence.

It is perfectly possible for scholars to manage the duality of high involvement with users and high independence from those same users. In doing double hurdle research it is important that we maintain the capacity for iconoclasm and challenge.

My own experience of working with people in business is that they are interested in ideas and concepts in their own right and that they are quite willing to be challenged with important ideas on important subjects.

ABOUT THE AUTHOR
Andrew Pettigrew is Dean of the University of Bath School of Management in the UK, Vice-President of EFMD and a noted researcher into the human, political, and social aspects of organisational strategy.

gf

Section_03
Rigour-Relevance and Business School Impact

"Asking questions about impact is, of course, a good way to communicate with stakeholders, but it is also a way to create an impact culture among all staff whether they be in an administrative or a teaching and research function"

Michel Kalika and Gordon Shenton
'Impact: is it enough just to talk about it?'

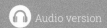 Audio version

Volume   Issue

13_01

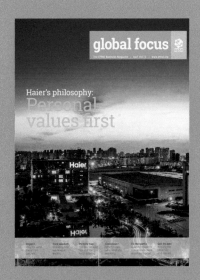

2018

Impact: is it enough just to talk about it?

Michel Kalika and **Gordon Shenton** explain why business schools not only talk about impact but are learning how to make a better job of assessing it

Business schools refer more and more frequently to the issue of impact when defining their mission/vision/strategy. In 2018, out of the 55 schools to which AACSB and EFMD board members belong, 42 (76%) use the terms "impact" or "influence" in defining their core purpose. Why is the concept of impact so present in business schools' current discourse?

We can put forward two major reasons. The first is the recurrent criticism that business schools are subjected to with regard to their legitimacy, particularly since the 2008 crisis. Giving prominence to their impact is one way of responding to this criticism.

The second corresponds to a paradigm change for business schools. For two long decades they had thrown themselves into a frantic race for international accreditation, which was the means for them to respond to the globalisation of the higher-education market and, of course, to improve the quality of their operations. Since the accreditation processes were aimed essentially at the way schools operate, on the organisation of their programmes and on the qualification of their faculty, the focus was primarily internal.

At present we are experiencing a paradigm shift for those schools, whose operations are now governed by international quality standards and by a growing concern for their contribution to external stakeholders in their home territory and in their home country.

The preoccupation with impact leads them to shift from a self-centred internal paradigm to a paradigm centred on business schools' externalities.

Moreover, the accreditation bodies have taken this change on board, AACSB having established impact as one of the three pillars of its system and EQUIS having included the concepts of impact and influence in its standards and criteria framework.

This being the case, the business schools cannot allow themselves to merely mention their impact in passing. They must clearly identify it, justify it and measure it. But it is here that a delicate problem appears: the concept of impact is multifaceted and multidimensional, while interpretations are diverse and measurement is complex. Faced with this complexity we believe that, for a business school, talking about impact entails answering three preliminary questions without which it will be hard to put something concrete behind the word and to get beyond the "impact washing" stage.

Q1 The first question is "the impact of what?"

Of course, we are talking about the business school as an undifferentiated whole that we need to define in terms of overall scope. But we must also determine for which of a school's activities we want to assess the impact. Is it the impact of the educational process on young students, the impact of executive education on practising managers or the impact of research?

Q2 The next question is "the impact on who?"

Is it on people (young students or managers), on companies or more generally on organisations? Or are we looking at the impact of a school on society at large?

Q3 Finally, when we talk about impact it is important to specify the impact zone involved: "the impact where?"

Is it the local environment (a city or a region)? Or is it a national territory or even a transnational area?

By answering these three questions we clarify the business school impact that is under consideration. If we combine the three questions, which each have three non-exclusive response modes, we have a three-dimensional matrix (see Figure 1).

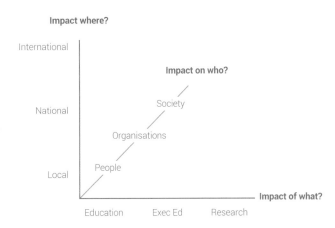

Figure 1

From our experience with BSIS on close to 40 campuses on three continents we can assert that the question of impact is far from being a simple question of communication ("impact washing") but is above all a strategic issue

Now let's take three examples of tools that can help us to better understand a school's impact.

• BSIS, which was created by the FNEGE in France and developed by the EFMD as an international service for its members, is a tool for evaluating a business school's impact on its home territory within a framework of seven dimensions (financial, educational, business development, intellectual, network, CSR, image). BSIS is concerned with educational activities at the pre- and post-experience levels and with research mainly for companies and organisations. Its scope is mostly local or regional. The system has been used on more that 35 campuses.

• The M Index was designed to assess the intellectual impact of a research centre and aims at measuring the impact of its research output (Q1) on companies (Q2) within a national territory (Q3). The assessment grid is made up of 20 criteria that cover the four stages of a research process: 1) The initial definition of the research project; 2) the execution of the research project; 3) the dissemination of the outcomes; and 4) the practical implementation of the outcomes in companies and organisations.

• The impact of courses on CSR on young students (Q1) would also be worth evaluating in terms of opinions and behaviour. In order to measure the impact of these courses one could imagine a survey tool addressed to students when they enter the business school, when they leave it and three years after their entry into the world of work, regardless of their geographical origin (Q3).

It is clear from these examples that the "discourse only" stage can be left behind and that business schools can equip themselves with tools to measure or better identify their impact.

Finally, from our experience with BSIS on close to 40 campuses on three continents we can assert that the question of impact is far from being a simple question of communication ("impact washing") but is above all a strategic issue.

Today many business schools are faced with two challenges of a strategic nature relating to impact.

The first challenge concerns the balance between local and global positioning. Many schools were created by and on a given territory in order to serve its need for trained managers to run its companies. In recent decades these same schools have centred their strategy on international development because of the globalisation of markets and accreditations.

The question of the balance between local impact and global impact is therefore squarely on the table and without any doubt business schools have an interest in showing their stakeholders that local impact is not opposed to global impact and that the latter often generates impact they were unaware of or had underestimated.

The second challenge lies in the balance between the academic and the managerial impact of research. Here the need to establish the recognition of management research alongside other scientific disciplines and the need to conform to accreditation criteria have pushed business schools to give preference to research that can be measured quantitatively by journal rankings, by their Impact Factor or by the H Index of the researchers. These publications certainly have an academic impact on the scientific community but their managerial impact on companies and organisations is limited.

We know that academic journals are not much read by managers. Moreover, since the incentives to publish rarely bear on the dissemination of their work, authors tend to direct their efforts towards

As we have just seen, measuring impact leads business schools to ask strategic questions regarding the positioning of their institution. It is important also to underline that the effort to better identify the external impact on companies and managers has an impact inside the business school itself.

Asking questions about impact is, of course, a good way to communicate with stakeholders, but it is also a way to create an impact culture among all staff whether they be in an administrative or a teaching and research function. BSIS has shown time and time again that it can be both a management tool and an instrument of change for business schools.

The authors would like to thank Martina Ticha for her help in the collection of data for the preparation of this article.

References

Parker, M. (2018). Shut Down the Business School. University of Chicago Press Economics Books.

https://www.aacsb.edu/blog/2018/august/the-power-of-global-business-school-networks-innovation-engagement-and-impact-at-work.

https://www.efmd.org/images/stories/efmd/EQUIS/2018/EQUIS_Standards_and_Criteria.pdf.

C. Lejeune & al., *The impact of business schools: Increasing the range of strategic choices*, Management International, Vol. 23 n°3, 2018.

https://efmdglobal.org/assessments/bsis/

https://www.researchgate.net/publication/328134022_The_Assessment_of_the_Managerial_Impact_of_Research_the_M_Index

the production of research output rather than on the communication of their findings.

However, rising research costs cause stakeholders to question business school managers about the usefulness and managerial impact of this research. This being said, we do not believe that academic impact and managerial impact are mutually exclusive.

An increase in the managerial impact of research upon managers can be achieved in two ways. On the one hand greater efforts must be made to translate research outcomes (by which we mean make scientific publications comprehensible) and to communicate these outcomes (newsletters, conferences, articles in professional journals, videos and so on.). On the other hand, the managerial impact can be increased by encouraging action research or intervention research that have an immediate impact upon companies.

About the Authors

Michel Kalika is Co-Director BSIS, EFMD Global Network

Gordon Shenton is Co-director BSIS and Senior Advisor, Quality Services, EFMD

Section_03
Rigour-Relevance and Business School Impact

"IMD's BSIS experience has been unequivocally positive. We entered into this process with a few hopes, all of which were fulfilled"

IMD
'Real learning, Real impact'

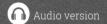 Audio version

Volume

Issue

14_02

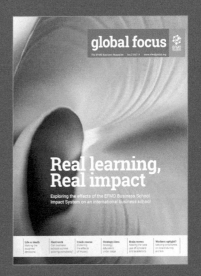

2020

Real learning,
Real impact

Jean-François Manzoni explores an international business
school's experience with the EFMD Business School Impact System

In 2017, IMD adopted the tagline "Real Learning, Real Impact," reflecting the institution's orientation towards having a significant and sustainable impact on individuals, organisations and society.

Around the same time, we were introduced to the EFMD Business School Impact System (BSIS), a systematic set of procedures for conducting an impact assessment. The presence of the word "impact" in the name initially caught our attention but that is not why we adopted the BSIS.

IMD committed to the BSIS for five main reasons.
• First, it was an opportunity to get done something we knew we ought to do but didn't necessarily find the time for. Understanding one's impact is important but not super urgent. Registering for BSIS was a way for us to put a deadline on the calendar and commit
• Second, we had some ideas on how to measure impact but honestly no one at IMD was a world-class expert in measuring all dimensions of impact. Some of us understood economic impact others academic impact, but none of us had thought about impact systemically for higher-education institutions. The BSIS folks had, so we said to ourselves: "Why reinvent the wheel if smart and dedicated experts have already spent a lot of time figuring this out?"
• Third, we figured that our assessment might be even more credible to our stakeholders if it was somehow "accredited" by an external, objective and expert party
• Fourth, our previous experience with accreditations suggested that comments of the peer review team are often very insightful and value creating. We hoped this would be true again
• Last, but not least, we thought that this BSIS assessment would give us a base line that we would be able to work with for years to come. This was a way for us to develop assessment skills that we could use again in the future, including to measure progress in key selected areas.

IMD began the BSIS data gathering in early 2019 and concluded the BSIS project with the release of a public-facing Impact Report in early 2020

Let us cut to the chase: IMD began the BSIS data gathering in early 2019 and concluded the BSIS project with the release of a public-facing Impact Report in early 2020. Our five objectives/hopes were all fulfilled. We also received the BSIS label in the process.

We look back on this journey as an extremely helpful one. We wanted to share our experience and outcomes, as it may help you decide whether engaging in the BSIS process is right for you.

Global reach

Following the end of the second world war in Europe, multinational companies were rapidly expanding and it was in this wave of globalisation that IMD's two predecessor management training schools were founded – IMEDE in Lausanne in 1956 and IMI in Geneva in 1947. They came together to form IMD three decades ago.

They were internationally diverse from day one, drawing faculty from North America and participants from across Europe. The language of instruction was English.

Since those founding periods, international diversity, global travel experiences and cross-cultural learning have come to define IMD. They are key to the transformative power of our learning experiences.

In 2018, EFMD EQUIS peer reviewers visiting the campus singled out internationalisation as a defining and distinguishing feature of the school.

Swiss Roots

While we continue to work hard at ensuring our "global reach," we are also very mindful – and proud – of our "Swiss roots".

These roots come in part from our founders – IMEDE was founded by Nestlé and IMI was strongly connected with Swiss companies. Over the years, IMD and its predecessors have been fortunate to have the support of many Swiss companies, several of whom are world leaders.

In addition to corporate connections, partnerships with world-class Swiss academic institutions have become a vital element of our educational offerings. Here, we have been plain lucky that we are surrounded by world-class institutions such as the École Polytechnique Fédérale de Lausanne (EPFL), ranked among the best universities in the world, and ECAL (Lausanne University of Art and Design), often ranked among the world's best design and art schools.

In particular, we partner with EPFL to offer TransformTECH, a five-day tech-infused bootcamp for executives.

In the research area, we are fortunate to have the support of several Swiss benefactors. IMD is also deeply engaged in the Swiss innovation economy. Since 1998, more than 400 Swiss start-ups have benefitted from the support of MBAs and EMBAs engaged in experiential learning Start-up Projects.

Finally, our Alumni Community for Entrepreneurship Lausanne Chapter facilitates "Start-up Nights" where local alumni learn about Swiss start-ups and how to invest in them.

New learnings on local impact

Through the BSIS process, we improved our understanding of IMD's impact overall and particularly in the Canton de Vaud in Switzerland. The 120 prompts comprising the BSIS assessment scaffolded our explorations.

Here's a sampling of what we learned:
- Economic Impact: IMD contributed SF360 million to the economy in Vaud in 2018, as calculated using the EFMD BSIS methodology
- Overnight Accommodations: IMD was responsible for an estimated 40,000 overnight stays in Vaud in 2018

400

Since 1998, more than 400 Swiss start-ups have benefitted from the support of IMD's MBAs and EMBAs engaged in experiential learning Start-up Projects

32

Of Switzerland's Top 100 Start-Ups, as ranked by the website startup.ch; 32 had previously worked with IMD MBAs and/or EMBAs. Also, 13 of the 24 Vaud firms designated as "scale-ups" by a prominent start-up accelerator have been past participants in the Start-up Projects

• Start-Up Support: Of Switzerland's Top 100 Start-Ups, as ranked by the website startup.ch; 32 had previously worked with IMD MBAs and/or EMBAs. Also, 13 of the 24 Vaud firms designated as "scale-ups" by a prominent start-up accelerator have been past participants in the Start-up Projects.

• Corporate Connections: IMD led custom executive education programmes for nine of Switzerland's top 25 companies by sales over a three-year period

• Executive Education Enrolments: In 2019, 26% of open programme participants were from Switzerland

• MBAs: About 25% of MBA graduates have historically stayed in Switzerland after graduation

• EMBAs: Of our EMBAs, nearly half live in Switzerland, with about half of that cohort being Swiss nationals.

As part of the BSIS process, we asked external stakeholders for their perceptions of IMD. A letter from the cantonal administration volunteered: "IMD plays a major role in the academic landscape of our canton;" A senior executive from MindMaze, Switzerland's first unicorn, described IMD's global reach and reputation as adding to the "internationalisation" of the canton; the director of the canton's economic development agency added his commendation: "The school's alumni are a large and influential community of positive ambassadors".

These words of praise were gratifying, of course, but, maybe more importantly, they were also eye-opening for us. Indeed, one of the points highlighted by the BSIS journey is how little we knew about certain dimensions of our impact..

In fact, one of the insightful questions asked by the BSIS expert visitors was "why is IMD so modest about its impact?"

Well, one reason is that we didn't really know how much impact we had. Another, and again an important insight for us, is IMD's internalising of Swiss values. The culture of enterprises in Switzerland is not to boast. Organisations go about their activities without spending too much time self-congratulating .

The BSIS process helped us realise that this Swiss discretion should not prevent us from objectively and calmly communicating our achievements and impact to external parties, including governments, of course, but also our own alumni.

Strengthening ecosystem partnerships

Another thoughtful suggestion from the BSIS peer review team was to intensify our interactions and co-operation with neighbouring academic institutions. As mentioned above we had started to do so. Their encouragement was hence timely and helpful.

Since their visit we launched a new tri-partite collaboration with EPFL and the University of Lausanne (UNIL). The new centre, called Enterprise for Society (E4S), will focus on the challenges and opportunities of technology-based innovation and promote dialogue between researchers and practitioners working with technology and those focusing on socio-economic issues to solve some of the world's greatest challenges.

The second pillar of E4S will be a more cohesive and synergistic approach of the three partners toward the region's entrepreneurial ecosystem, which already features numerous successful start-ups but could do even more.

Last but not least, we will be launching a joint pre-experience master's degree in sustainable management and technology.

Learning from the BSIS experts

When we began the BSIS process, we had clear intentions to share our findings with the cantonal and local government. We had not really thought about what form this communication would take but I think we all assumed it would be like everything we do at IMD – in English.

The BSIS expert visitors helped us realise that while IMD works internationally and almost exclusively in English, the language of the canton in which our main campus is French, one of Switzerland's four national languages.

Yes, we know, we knew that, but somehow, we had never realised how annoying our language policy must have been for local politicians

During a recent meeting, the mayor of Lausanne expressed his pleasant surprise at the size of IMD's local financial impact. He had simply no idea it was that high. Since then we have continued to take the language and the local connection lesson to heart and we have been communicating more of our research, thought leadership and campus news in French

Extending our impact

One lesson of IMD's BSIS experience is that in the balance between localisation and globalisation in business schools, it does not have to be one way or the other; it can be both.

International business schools, no matter how globally diverse their faculty, students and programmes, have numerous local interdependencies and are inherently local institutions.

At IMD our educational activities forge a path that draws from both the local ecosystem and from international diversity. Such an approach has been transformative for all participants — those from Switzerland and those from abroad.

Even as many face-to-face programmes have transitioned to remote learning during the COVID-19 crisis, we are still a "global meeting place" – just that the meeting place can also be on Canvas and Zoom.

The BSIS experience showed us that measuring and assessing one's local impact can be a catalyst for fortifying local collaborations.

IMD's BSIS experience has been unequivocally positive. We entered into this process with a few hopes, described at the start of this article, all of which were fulfilled. The process also led us to a few key realisations, which are already having a non-trivial impact on the way we approach some topics. In particular, it helped us to understand better the need to balance local and international impact.

We are grateful to Michel Kalika and his colleague on the review team Robert Galliers for their supportive challenges and insights.

gf

The penny had never dropped.

It finally did when the expert visitors challenged us on it.

In January 2020, we released our BSIS findings in a 44-page Impact Report that was published in both English and French (*Rapport d'Impact*). The publication date coincided with the announcement by EFMD of the awarding of the BSIS label.

The report piqued the interest of several local stakeholders. One top Canton de Vaud official commented: "The BSIS project demonstrates the positive impact of IMD and the school's integration into the Vaud economic fabric".

During a recent meeting, the mayor of Lausanne expressed his pleasant surprise at the size of IMD's local financial impact. He had simply no idea it was that high. Since then we have continued to take the language and the local connection lesson to heart and we have been communicating more of our research, thought leadership and campus news in French. We are also working on a regular French language newsletter.

This is an important development because positive relations with various levels of governments and other local stakeholders are critical to IMD's long-term aspirations in areas such as national accreditation, land use, fundraising and research support.

44pp

In January 2020, IMD released its BSIS findings in a 44 page Impact Report that was published in both English and French (*Rapport d'Impact*). The publication date coincided with the announcement by EFMD of the awarding of the BSIS label

About the Author

Jean-François Manzoni is President of IMD

Anne-France Borgeaud Pierazzi is Institutional Research and Accreditations Partner

Eric Neutuch is Accreditation and Institutional Projects Officer

gf

Section_03
Rigour-Relevance and Business School Impact

"Going through BSIS has been very beneficial for St Gallen, as it brings a well defined and structured process for developing new instruments and for providing data on the important strategic challenges that our 'industry' faces"

Thomas Bieger
'How being embedded in your region helps growth'

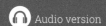 Audio version

Volume   Issue

08_03

2014

HOW BEING EMBEDDED IN YOUR REGION HELPS GROWTH

 THOMAS BIEGER

EXPLAINS HOW THE UNIVERSITY OF ST GALLEN USED
THE NEW BUSINESS SCHOOL IMPACT SURVEY TO
CONSOLIDATE AND BUILD ON ITS LOCAL ROOTS

Imagine you are the chief executive of an airport whose customers are rather dispersed. Some of them live up to 100 miles away, which is true of a minimum of 40% of hub transfer passengers.

Your main concern is your airport's international positioning against the major hubs and their worldwide competition. Your main markets are international transfer passengers and international airlines. You therefore recruit top staff and specialists from an increasingly competitive international labour market.

However, access to local resources is key for the expansion of your airport, the local labour market, rail and road access, subsidies for those public services that your airport delivers and the development of neighbouring businesses.

Simultaneously, the regional environment sees the negative impacts, such as direct externalities like noise; and many locals regard indirect externalities, such as the role of the airport as a representation of globalisation, as a threat.

Many companies with operations fixed to a specific location face similar challenges. They compete in international markets but have to combine their international reach – even their global reach – with their local and regional roots. They rely on local resources and regional and national laws regulate them.

The same is true of business schools – not just traditional, campus schools but also multi-campus universities and virtual business schools offering pure e-learning products. All of them need to nurture their local roots. For example, they need at least a legal local base to ensure accreditation. Further, they draw on the brand and image of their home base.

"

Many companies with operations fixed to a specific location rely on local resources and regional and national laws regulate them

Compared to other institutions of higher education, business schools face a specific challenge regarding caring about this local "embeddedness" because:

- their graduates work for global companies and not for the regional economy and society as do most medical doctors, lawyers and teachers that traditional comprehensive universities produce
- to achieve their global ambition, they rely on the professors and leadership that the global faculty market provides
- from the public's point of view they are often those responsible for bad management practices and are even the source of economic crises. This is most predominant in respect of the best business schools in a country with a dominant market share. Many view these schools as embodying an ever-present risk that their alumni will feature in tomorrow's negative headlines about incompetent managers.

All of the above are reasons why the University of St Gallen in Switzerland has undertaken the Business School Impact Survey (BSIS) assessment process offered by EFMD Global Network and FNEGE (French National Foundation for Management Education).

The University of St Gallen's vision is to establish and further its position in the worldwide university landscape. However, 20% of its overall financial budget originates from its region, the Canton of St Gallen, while only 10% of its students do.

As one of 10 state universities in Switzerland, it is the only specialised university whose graduates, unlike those of the universities of Basel and Zurich, leave the region, with only a small minority remaining. Sixty-four per cent of its faculty are non-Swiss and only 5% originate directly from from the Canton of St.Gallen.

40%

Airport customers are rather dispersed, some of them live up to 100 miles away, which is true of a minimum of 40% of hub transfer passengers

20%

20% of the University of St Gallen's overall financial budget originates from its region, the Canton of St Gallen, while only 10% of its students do

Moreover, in the aftermath of the global financial crises, St Gallen – like all the leading business schools in Europe – is perceived in terms of the failure of a few of its thousands of graduates in leading management positions. The university is thus criticised as one of those mainly responsible for the economic problems during the crisis years.

By producing an extensive self-evaluation report as part of the BSIS process the university not only clarified the impact measurement criteria but also developed them further. The clear structure of the report template has allowed a thorough internal review of the university's goals and strategy.

More importantly, the two-day onsite BSIS peer review allowed reflection on the entire embeddedness management process. Interviews with local stakeholders provided an independent review of all of the university's links, which allowed new ideas for actions and strategic adjustments to emerge.

Embeddedness is defined as "the way in which organisations or actors become tied into the local business and institutional environment" (see Alderman 2004 in Kern-Ulmer 2011 p26).

Embeddedness not only encompasses different layers of links and processes (social, political, economic; see Hayter 2004), but also of logistical/technical processes. However, this embeddedness cannot be delegated to political lobbies. Integration into regional value networks is as important as the visibility and the integration of a school's representatives, its leadership and its professors in the region's social networks.

Multi-campus operations have to take the different cultural and institutional contexts (see North 1990, ...humanly devised constraints that shape human interaction) into account, since the type and level of integration expected need to vary. Most importantly, the various stakeholders, who mostly represent local resources, must also be acknowledged.

For business schools these stakeholders could comprise regional/national regulation and accreditation authorities, the regional student market (students act as multipliers to the broader society), civil interest groups, public authorities in charge of infrastructure such as transport and construction authorities, the regional labour market, local suppliers and service partners, and location marketing associations.

Embeddedness and strategies related to it are important moderators of the value creation processes (see Kern-Ulmer 2011). Like any strategic activity, embeddedness needs an approach inspired by the familiar management cycles of measuring, planning, acting and controlling.

Consequently, long time horizons and a relational approach are crucial. Purely transactional activities with a short perspective, such as information and lobbying campaigns before a construction project starts, are very often perceived as opportunistic and may even be counterproductive in the longer term.

Extensive indicators need to be defined to monitor a business school's regional impact. Impact measurement should therefore not only encompass traditional economic dimensions such as the regional value added (in the University of St Gallen's case, 1 SFR of regional public money converts into a regional income of 5 SFR). However, a purely economic perspective can easily be seen as only transactional and tactical.

Social interlinks can be divided into direct links to core processes, such as the number of projects and graduate placements with regional companies, and more general, indirect ones, such as employees' links with regional organisations, the number of hours they spend as volunteers in regional associations and so on.

"

Embeddedness implies full integration into not only regional social and economic networks but also political and technical ones. A purely transactions level is not sufficient

200

University of St Gallen faculty have active supervisory or management roles in more than 200 companies and foundations listed in the Swiss Commercial Register and approximately 40% of these are located within the region

University of St Gallen faculty have active supervisory or management roles in more than 200 companies and foundations listed in the Swiss Commercial Register and approximately 40% of these are located within the region.

There are also other important impacts, such as an organisation's image and its contributions to local/regional brands.

Nevertheless, the negative impacts in each dimension also need to be considered, for example a business school's influence on the local real estate market and rents, traffic, loss of regional identity and others.

As mentioned, embeddedness implies full integration into not only regional social and economic networks but also political and technical ones. A purely transactions level is not sufficient.

General corporate social responsibility concepts (see Social Responsibilities of Business Corporations 1971) can inspire and define embeddedness goals at different levels. For example, an operation can be:

- compliant, in the sense that it fulfils all the legal requirements of its regional links
- responsible, by accepting additional remits
- responsive, by taking a proactive role and, taking all its relevant positive and negative impacts into account, trying to influence the region's systems positively

The University of St Gallen operationalised its embeddedness goal as "the university is not only seen as a factor of regional benefits but as an important factor of regional life" (a relational and not only a transactional perspective). A related instrumental goal was "every citizen at least indirectly has an access or direct contact as employer, speaker, visitor, supplier, friend to a unit or representative of the university".

Measures such as presenting public events, delivering not only public lectures, but also comprehensive programmes, acting as a point of contact for regional SMEs, contributing to regional events by means of faculty and staff presentations and organising decentralised stakeholder meetings (round tables) are important.

The overarching goal is to assure long-term access to local resources such as the local labour market, the student housing market, efficient local suppliers, to be socially and politically accepted and to be perceived as legitimate in order to enjoy long-term political support in budget discussions or for upcoming construction projects.

An additional goal is to develop the location's competitive position, especially its industrial clusters, quality of life and its local brand.

In this process, outside views allowing reflection on an organisation's approach are helpful, a key role of BSIS.

Since the entire management education industry, like any other operation with a fixed location, faces similar challenges, the exchange of know-how in the BSIS scheme is of real value. In addition, boards and local politicians want to be sure that the university management links properly with its environment. The external legitimation of a university's embeddedness activities is therefore compulsory.

Going through BSIS has been very beneficial for the school, as it brings a well defined and structure process for developing new instruments and for providing data on the important strategic challenges that our "industry" faces.

FURTHER INFORMATION

If you would like further information or are interested in your school taking part in BSIS please contact: Gordon Shenton gordon.shenton@efmdglobal.org, Michel Kalika michel.kalika@efmdglobal.org or bsis@efmdglobal.org

ABOUT THE AUTHOR

Thomas Bieger is President, University of St Gallen, Switzerland

Section_03
Rigour-Relevance and Business School Impact

"The most important story we discovered through the BSIS process was not one of facts and figures. It was the story of ourselves. It was the story of a business school in a small province in transition"

Sobey Business School
'Creating impact with purpose'

 Audio version

Volume   Issue

11_02

2017

Patricia Bradshaw and Erin Elaine Casey describe how the
BSIS process has helped herald the impact of the Sobey School in
Canada, the first business school in North America to utilise the system

Creating impact with purpose

Our location between the Atlantic Ocean and the continent can be described as "liminal space"; a threshold between what came before and what is next or a transition that involves waiting but not knowing. As with many business schools, we are situated in a precarious place, welcoming the world to our campus and knowing that change is coming but uncertain about what that change will involve

The Sobey School of Business at Saint Mary's University is a large business school in a medium-sized university in a small city in a small province on the far eastern coast of Canada.

We think of our city and province as a welcoming gateway, much in the way that Ellis Island was in the US. Over the early decades of our history, immigrants to Canada landed by boat at Pier 21 in Halifax and travelled to other parts of the country.

Our location between the Atlantic Ocean and the continent can be described as "liminal space"; a threshold between what came before and what is next or a transition that involves waiting but not knowing. As with many business schools, we are situated in a precarious place, welcoming the world to our campus and knowing that change is coming but uncertain about what that change will involve.

The instability of our particular location is captured by the trends outlined in the *Now or Never: An Urgent Call to Action for All Nova Scotians* 2014 report (https://onens.ca/commission-report/) on the dire economic and demographic challenges facing our province. The report's authors urged all sectors in the province to undertake collective action to address a declining population, outward migration of young people, poor economic performance, decline of rural areas and high dependence on government support.

The report recognises universities as important drivers of change to help reverse these trends. For example, universities can attract international students and encourage some of them to stay in the region. We can incubate and accelerate start-ups that grow the economy. We can drive entrepreneurship, innovation and leadership to enhance productivity and support international trade and the development of global mindsets embedded in values of sustainability and corporate social responsibility.

In their 2011 article "Collective Impact" in the winter edition of the *Stanford Social Innovation Review* John Kania and Mark Kramer described the difference between isolated and collective impact.

With isolated impact, single organisations formulate independent solutions to complex problems. While they might make progress, it tends to be limited rather than systemic.

Collective impact, on the other hand, involves a long-term commitment by a number of influential people and groups to make significant change. No organisation can single-handedly solve any major social problem. Ideally, such change is guided by shared goals and measurement systems, collaborative and complementary activities, and clear communication.

At the Sobey School of Business, we felt compelled to be a partner for prosperity, keeping in mind the call for a collective impact approach. We knew that our impact would be limited if we acted in isolation from community partners. We also recognised the need for cross-sector coalitions that commit, over the long term, to a common agenda to change how we build prosperity and a healthy future.

21

We think of our city and province as a welcoming gateway, over the early decades of our history, immigrants to Canada landed by boat at Pier 21 in Halifax and travelled to other parts of the country

We wanted to benchmark our contributions and build our reputation as a partner in collective action in an accountable and transparent way. Using the Business School Impact System (BSIS), we were able to learn from others' experiences and test our assumptions about our contributions.

BSIS is designed to determine the extent of a school's impact upon its local environment and was initially designed by FNEGE (the French National Foundation for Management Education) and is already well established in the French higher-education arena.

The process has now been adapted for an international audience and is offered in a joint venture between EFMD and FNEGE as a service to EFMD members in any part of the world.

Internally, the BSIS process at Sobey became an opportunity for reflection, data collection, dialogue and commitment to working together with purpose. Externally, it was an opportunity to build our brand as a contributor to regional prosperity and success.

We are the first business school in North America to undertake the BSIS and the process gave us a number of insights. Perhaps the most exciting is the determination that the Sobey School of Business, with our 3,200 students, makes a direct, indirect and induced annual economic contribution to the Nova Scotia economy of $329 million. Eighty-seven per cent of our budget is spent in the province.

We also determined that:

- Every year, more than one-third of our undergraduates and two-thirds of our graduate students stay, work and help to build the prosperity of the region on completing their programmes
- In one year, our chapter of the international ENACTUS movement, with a membership of more than 200 students, launched 34 businesses, created 156 jobs, helped 447 refugees and provided 2,300 kilograms of food to hungry people
- The Sobey School Business Development Centre works with 700 students annually to utilise design thinking aimed at creating start-ups. This includes the Startup 100 Project, which helped more than 100 students create 100 new ventures in 50 communities
- More than 45% of our 78 faculty members are involved in community organisations, including various governance roles

87%

Eighty-seven per cent of our budget is spent in the province – Sobey School of Business, with our 3,200 students, makes a direct, indirect and induced annual economic contribution to the Nova Scotia economy of $329 million

BSIS has helped us articulate a much stronger sense of brand, pride and identity both internally and externally. It has identified and spurred dialogue about common goals within our business school and university and with our colleagues and neighbours outside them

45%

More than 45% of our 78 faculty members are involved in community organisations, including various governance roles

- The Sobey School is ranked 11th in the world by Corporate Knights Better World MBA Rankings and 75% of faculty teach and/or research in the area of corporate social responsibility
- We train 1,800 managers in professional and executive learning programmes annually
- Our activities support the province's new China strategy. Each year, the school recruits approximately 100 undergraduate and 70 masters students from China. Twenty faculty members fly to China every year to teach in our joint Bachelor of Commerce programme with Beijing Normal University of Zhuhai
- In 2014, our faculty published 21 peer-reviewed articles and four cases, wrote seven book chapters, produced 11 reports and gave 39 conference presentations on topics directly influencing our region.
- Through our research centres, we shared knowledge with over 1,000 participants at 15 public talks, conferences and seminars

BSIS helped us assemble a catalogue of accomplishments of which we feel extremely proud. It helped us understand that we can do an even better job of benchmarking and measuring our successes, of encouraging and highlighting collaboration and interdisciplinary endeavours within the school and across the university, of tracking our commitment to social responsibility, and of telling each other and the community how and what we are doing.

Reaching out is changing our school culture and stimulating new projects. New faculty are attracted to our mission and story, resulting in positive momentum and a growing wellspring of energy and sense of empowerment. While still living in that liminal space and experiencing that sense of precariousness, we are more confident in our ability to tolerate uncertainty.

Feedback from outside the university reinforces this positive feeling. For example, in November of 2016 the Nova Scotia Minister of Business recognised our work with a motion of

congratulations in the Legislature. The motion noted, in part, that "the Sobey School of Business at Saint Mary's University delivers top quality graduates every year and is an important asset to both Nova Scotia's academic and business communities..."

Going forward, this enhanced understanding of ourselves means we can better anticipate and respond to needs in the community. The generosity of that community in participating in the BSIS process revealed their faith in our ability to respond to challenges. They told us that we have an established and solid place in the social and economic ecosystem. This is both a challenge and an opportunity.

Saint Mary's University has long existed in juxtaposition to several other universities in the province, and has had a tendency to define itself in terms of what it is not. The BSIS has helped us articulate a much stronger sense of brand, pride and identity both internally and externally. It has identified and spurred dialogue about common goals within our business school and university and with our colleagues and neighbours outside them. Each of us is still doing what we do best. And we are now also consciously working collectively.

The most important story we discovered through the BSIS process was not one of facts and figures. It was the story of ourselves. It was the story of a business school in a small province in transition. We inhabit an important gateway. We are on the edge and – if we have anything to say about it – the edge of a new era of prosperity, growth and hope.

To read our* Creating Impact With Purpose First Impact Report, *visit https://www.smu.ca/ webfiles/BSIS_FullReport_WEB.pdf.***

ABOUT THE AUTHORS

Dr Patricia Bradshaw is Dean of the Sobey School of Business at Saint Mary's University in Halifax, Nova Scotia, Canada. patricia.bradshaw@smu.ca.

Erin Casey is a writer and partner in collective action in the province.

Section_03
Rigour-Relevance and Business School Impact

"We must raise the profile and positive impact of management education, scholarship and the institutions that provide them if we are to avoid future economic calamity, restore confidence and strengthen public trust"

Laurent Batsch et al
'Growing the impact of management education and scholarship'

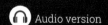 Audio version

Volume Issue

10_01

2015

Growing the impact of management education and scholarship

Management is not only taught in business schools. For more than 100 years it has also been taught by a special type of university that is 'more than a business school'. An international group of university leaders trace the emergence, role and future contributions of 'universities for business and management'

Some traditions remain vital while others are fading. The various traditions of opera, for example, maintain their rich heritage, yet have evolved and synthesised with new developments to extend and broaden their appeal. International ensemble casts perform across the globe. Sets and costumes incorporate designs inspired by different cultures and new technologies. Some observers attribute opera's revitalisation partly to Luciano Pavarotti, Jose Carerras and Placido Domingo, who banded together to form the "Three Tenors" back in the 1990s.

Performing traditional and modern opera pieces at large concert venues, this pluralistic approach expanded popular appreciation of great composers, such as Wagner and Bizet. The Three Tenors operatic renditions reached out to and resonated with new and existing audiences in cities around the world: Tokyo, Sao Paolo, Seoul, Pretoria and Beijing – the list goes on.

The future of management education and scholarship

Just like opera, management education needs to balance tradition and innovation. Clearly, it is transforming its delivery and learning techniques to embrace new possibilities offered by technology and digitalisation. But is it being enriched by a renaissance of its own?

Many undergraduate business programmes remain too narrow and focused on management techniques and theories. But corporate leaders want management graduates with the ability to look beyond the obvious, to question assumptions, to be more creative – to understand how business is *a part of* society and not *apart from* society.

Few institutions continually experiment with preparing students for innovation, entrepreneurial thinking or navigating a business environment set in a global world that is culturally diverse, yet highly connected. Fewer institutions are committed to preparing graduate and undergraduate students to discharge their duties to society responsibly. There are serious implications to how the next generation of business leaders are cultivated.

The 2007-08 Financial Crisis, precipitated by gross corporate mismanagement and greed, eroded society's confidence in business school graduates to dangerous lows. Indeed, the 2011 *Rethinking undergraduate business education* report by the Carnegie Foundation for the

Advancement of Teaching highlighted this worrying perception held by the public.

Sophisticated students around the world, organised through social media networks such as the Post-Crash Economics Society, are demanding that management syllabi be rethought to equip them to make a better world - and not just deliver better short-term returns to shareholders at the expense of other legitimate stakeholders.

Industry and research funders should heed the type of "socially responsible scholarship" that bridges the science-practice gap described by Ann S Tsui in "Reconnecting with the business world" (*Global Focus*, 2015). We must raise the profile and positive impact of management education, scholarship and the institutions that provide them if we are to avoid future economic calamity, restore confidence and strengthen public trust.

Before embarking on this journey, it may be useful to first survey some history of management education.

A diverse ecosystem for growth and sustainability

Comprehensive universities, dating back as early as 11th century Bologna, and technological universities, which developed in response to engineering and scientific needs in the 19th century, are among the earliest examples of educational institutions that have adapted to meet the changing needs of their times. Over time, such progressive universities expanded into the nascent social sciences, later on into economics and finally into management. As management education grew in significance, a spectrum of new institutions emerged.

Existing comprehensive and technological universities evolved to include management faculties and business schools. On the furthest end of this part of the spectrum are the independent business schools focusing almost entirely on graduate and executive education. What then lies at the other end of this spectrum?

Since the end of the 19th century, a third type of University emerged to meet globalisation's imperative for Universities to provide an integrated understanding of different cultures, law, and various management techniques such as accounting, marketing, communications and so on. Some of these began as schools of commerce, and developed into what could be termed

> "
>
> *Managers cannot ignore the deep philosophical undercurrents running through the history of mankind and across cultures – they must understand and take into consideration how their decisions affect and are affected by our interconnected social fabrics*

"Universities for Business and Management". Later institutions were conceived as specialised universities from the outset. Examples are the University of St. Gallen or Wirtschaftsuniversität Vienna (both founded in 1898), the Copenhagen Business School (1917), Renmin University of China (1937) and later on Université Paris Dauphine (1969) and Singapore Management University (2000). These institutions were often initiated in collaboration with trade associations. Others, like Hitotsubashi University (1875) were founded by patriotic statesmen.

Although these universities differ in terms of the learning experience they provide students, they all – without exception – embrace inter-, multi- and trans-disciplinary curricula. They share the understanding that the classical business school disciplines should be enriched and cross-reinforced by the broader social sciences and humanities, e.g. law, political science, socio-economics, geography, communication, anthropology, psychology, foreign languages; as well as by science, technology and mathematics.

These universities tend to have strong engagement with practitioners, public agencies and civil society; and inform professionals, practitioners and policy-makers of the latest research findings. Compared to technological universities and engineering schools, these Management Universities integrate quantitative skills with a social science perspective. And unlike comprehensive universities, they do not "silo" their management schools into largely autonomous faculties - and thus avoid treating these as isolated and rather technical disciplines. A systematic integration of related sciences in the form of strong departments or highly interconnected schools in these Management Universities is what distinguishes them from pure Business Schools.

Stronger institutions to grow society's trust

Managers cannot ignore the deep philosophical undercurrents running through the history of mankind and across cultures. If business is to truly be *a part of* society, then managers must understand and take into consideration how their decisions affect and are affected by our interconnected social fabrics. These are ancient ideas.

Aristotle's prescience in matters of political economy was noted by Malcolm Macintosh in "Re-organising the Political Economy" (Global Focus, 2015). Aristotle also advocated *phronesis* as an intellectual virtue that is "reasoned and capable of action with regard to things that are good or bad for man".

In early Western civilization, *phronesis* was recognised as that activity by which the analytical and instrumental rationality of *episteme* and *techne* is balanced by value-rationality. *Phronesis* would require business leaders to look beyond profits and growth as ends in themselves and better honour the trust bestowed by society.

Ancient eastern philosophy deeply influenced E F Schumacher, a protégé of John Maynard Keynes, who had advised the government of Myanmar (formerly Burma). In a collection of essays, *Small is beautiful: a study of economics as if people mattered*, Schumacher expressed the function of work as giving people opportunities to utilise and develop their faculties; to overcome their ego-centeredness by joining in common tasks; and to bring forth the goods and services needed for a meaningful human existence.

More recently, in *Securing the future of management education* (2014), Howard Thomas and Michelle Lee from the Singapore Management University and their co-authors have advocated nurturing "a holistic student perspective on management (not a silo-oriented one) that will encourage the development of integrative thinkers who, in management careers, will be more likely to make decisions with integrity, reflection, and an ethical and moral compass".

Ulrike Landfester, from the University of St Gallen, had noted in 2013 (during a workshop on "Humanities and Social Sciences in Management

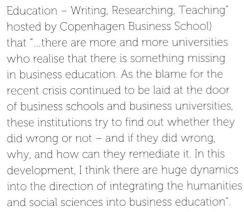

Traditional business disciplines provide a challenging context for social science and humanities scholars to engage the key economic, political and managerial questions of our time; and influence the education of future leaders in our economy

Education – Writing, Researching, Teaching" hosted by Copenhagen Business School) that "...there are more and more universities who realise that there is something missing in business education. As the blame for the recent crisis continued to be laid at the door of business schools and business universities, these institutions try to find out whether they did wrong or not – and if they did wrong, why, and how can they remediate it. In this development, I think there are huge dynamics into the direction of integrating the humanities and social sciences into business education".

Thoughts like these prove that a broader view on common issues at hand can generate inspiring new ideas. At the specialised universities, scholars from the social sciences, humanities and adjacent disciplines collaborate with, challenge and inspire their colleagues in the traditional business disciplines.

Traditional business disciplines provide a challenging context for social science and humanities scholars to engage the key economic, political and managerial questions of our time; and influence the education of future leaders in our economy.

This integration simultaneously gives these institutions some of the vitality of liberal arts colleges and the robustness of esteemed centuries-old comprehensive universities. Such integration revitalises fundamental and highly pertinent questions about the interdependence of business, markets, technology, culture and politics. It also ensures a broad set of intellectual explorations and educational capacities. For example, a good strategy consultant has to understand how technological and cultural shifts impact the regulatory landscape; a financial adviser has to understand markets and therefore the psychology of market actors.

This integration of adjacent disciplines helps ensure the continued societal relevance and responsibility of management scholarship as the world transforms.

Certain universities go beyond preparing young adults for professional or entry-level roles in today's workforce. Such universities aspire to nurture active change makers who can help transform society, not just observe or analyse passively

Contributing to the development of management education

Beyond honouring society's trust and strengthening themselves as meaningful individual institutions, the aggregation and collaboration of Management Universities present tremendous possibilities. They have the collective potential to innovate and tangibly amplify the profile and impact of management education and scholarship for society by:

1. Pursuing synergies across interdisciplinary education, research and practice-relevant scholarship by artfully enlisting technology

These universities enlist the social sciences to help re-contextualise management scholarship and enhance local and practical relevance. Each university makes a unique contribution through deep integration of its own adjacent disciplinary strengths such as the humanities, public policy and information science.

Complementary research disciplines also bridge quantitative and qualitative methodology, and their close relationships with practitioners enable researchers to collaborate and pursue high-impact interdisciplinary research projects. The possibilities promise to be distinct from, yet complementary to, the types of projects pursued by larger comprehensive universities. For example, researchers at Université Paris Dauphine's LAMSADE, a CNRS-funded computer science and decision analytics research institute; and Singapore Management University's School of Information Systems have begun an ambitious exploration of how analytics can inform appropriate organisational policies that support positive business changes, more effective consumer marketing and better urban living.

Innovations in learning form a major focus of their pedagogy. These universities display a deep commitment to innovative management education and experiment with next-practices

related to technology-enabled learning or nurturing, future-ready mindsets and competencies. They go beyond preparing young adults for professional or entry-level roles in today's workforce. Such universities aspire to nurture active change makers who can help transform society, not just observe or analyse passively.

2. Enhancing engagement with stakeholders and contribute to local and regional social and economic life

Through the design of their campuses, programmes and partnerships, these universities embrace their inherent "embeddedness" within the community and region, and pursue long-term trust-filled relationships with stakeholders.

The hard-to-quantify social and economic externalities they provide are felt and communicated by word-of-mouth testimonials. Each of these universities appreciates the importance of supporting local and regional companies with talent, and encourages students to serve and be part of the community through project-based work, volunteering and other initiatives. The University of St Gallen in Switzerland, which underwent the Business School Impact Survey offered by the EFMD Global Network and the French National Foundation for Management Education (*Global Focus*, 2014), seeks to embody this ethos.

3. Enhancing the global mind-set and profile for students, faculty and the institution

Management Universities generate possibilities for international collaboration and synergy distinct from the environment within any large comprehensive university given their common ethos and commitment to innovation, relevance and social responsibility. One example is the Singapore Management University-Copenhagen Business School structured bachelor exchange around Maritime Economics and International Shipping, which seeks to leverage and nurture special expertise within the context and practice

of each university's region, network of industry practitioners, government agencies and organisations; while paving the way for joint research and a host of other partnerships.

Uncovering new value and sustainability for all

Mirroring the Three Tenors, emergent Management Universities, working together with business schools, could achieve "innovation within tradition". They will help develop broader conceptions of effective and socially responsible education, and high-impact management research and scholarship. They will also further our understanding of how individual and organisational actors are embedded in their social environments, and how this shapes their repertoire of actions.

Management education is denied its due merit when narrowly perceived as mostly a private good. Management Universities around the world are poised to amplify the recognition and appreciation of all our institutions as trusted creators, protectors and purveyors of both public value and private goods for society.

ABOUT THE AUTHORS

Laurent Batsch is President, Universite Paris Dauphine, France;
Thomas Bieger is President, University of St Gallen, Switzerland;
Arnoud De Meyer is President, Singapore Management University, Singapore;
Per Holten-Andersen is President, Copenhagen Business School, Denmark;
Sriven Naidu is Director of Strategic Planning, Singapore Management University, Singapore;
Arnaud Raynouard is Vice-President, International Affairs, Universite Paris Dauphine, France;
Dorte Salskov-Iversen is Vice-President, International Affairs, Copenhagen Business School, Denmark;
Flavio Vasconcelos is Director, FGV-EBAPE (Brazilian School of Public and Business Administration), Brazil

Section_03
Rigour-Relevance and Business School Impact

"All parties in the research enterprise can contribute to the pursuit of socially responsible scholarship by remembering the goal of science: the discovery and application of true knowledge to improve the human condition"

Anne S Tsui
'Reconnecting with the business world: Socially Responsible Scholarship'

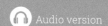 Audio version

Volume   Issue

09_01

2014

Anne S Tsui suggests how business school scholars can overcome the growing criticism of irrelevant and self-serving research

Reconnecting with the business world

SOCIALLY RESPONSIBLE SCHOLARSHIP

For the past 25 years, business school research has been criticised for its serious disconnection from the world of business practice and for being an insulated and self-serving activity on the part of both school leadership and individual scholars.

These criticisms seem severe but collectively we, professors and doctoral students of business schools worldwide, are spending a lot of our time writing papers with unclear value for practice or perhaps even for knowledge. It seems that we have forgotten both the scientific and social mission of scholarship.

Some deans of business schools refer to research as the "paper production function". (A scholar used the term "machine shops" and another "Taylorising business school research".) In such scenarios, the faculty is the workforce in the paper production factories.

Then, there are the journals, which publish the papers written by the workers in these paper factories. Journal editors (who are usually esteemed senior "workers") use "workers" in different factories to judge the papers submitted to them in terms of theoretical and methodological rigour.

A third group, such as the *Financial Times*, *US News and World Report* or Thomson Reuters, which publishes the *Science Citation Index* and *Social Science Citation Index*, ranks the journals and the schools.

Research factories, journals and ranking publishers thus form the three legs of the research enterprise operating today.

Interestingly, practising managers, ostensibly the consumers of the "knowledge" supposedly produced, play no part unless they are needed as "research subjects". Researchers look to the papers published in the "top" journals for ideas to study. Their primary goal or motivation is not to help practising managers solve their problems but to garner approval from the editors and reviewers of the journals.

Journals and school rankings are important to business schools. Highly ranked schools attract the best students, outstanding scholars, research grants and endowments. Schools value the highly ranked journals because only these are counted in school rankings. Journals are ranked not by the topics they study or the practical relevance of the research but by the frequency of citations by other academic journals. The relevance of the content for management practice is largely inconsequential in the ranking formula.

However, evidence is mounting that publication in top academic journals is no guarantee that these articles are of high quality or relevance.

A 2012 study in the *Academy of Management Perspective* substantiates the research–practice gap. The study found that the names or ideas of 384 of the most cited, hence most respected, scholars rarely appear on Google.com websites or webpages that the general public, including managers, read. The authors conclude: "The science–practice gap does not seem to be narrowing".

Is it socially responsible to produce scholarship that provides no value for practice, especially scholarship in practice-oriented disciplines such as business and management? Is it socially responsible to apply valuable intellectual and financial resources to the paper production function for the sole purpose of improving school rankings?

The pressure to publish fuels questionable research practices in all scientific fields. A 2005 *Nature* article, "Scientists behaving badly," discusses the problem in the natural sciences. A 2010 article, "Management science on the credibility bubble: Cardinal sins and various misdemeanors," showed serious violations of research ethics such as withholding methodology details, selective reporting of results, using others' ideas without credit, dropping observations to improve statistical results and even fabricating results.

A *Science* article, "China's publication bazaar," reports that top journal publications are the tickets to financial rewards, promotion and occupational prestige, giving rise to an industry of "fake" authorships.

The *Science* editors investigated 27 agencies in China that advertised papers and authorship for sale, with the value of an authorship ranging from $1,600 to $26,000.

Even without direct monetary involvement, the "Management science credibility" study reported researchers join "article publication communes" to increase the number of papers. Eight in 10 respondents in this study had witnessed faculty inappropriately accepting or assigning authorship credit. Is it socially responsible scholarship to engage in these questionable research practices?

384

A 2012 study found that the names or ideas of 384 of the most cited, hence most respected, scholars rarely appear on Google.com websites or webpages

This production culture and a narrow journal list carry a third unintended consequence: the worldwide convergence of research paradigms. New ideas and new discoveries are lacking in a "homogenisation of scholarship".

Most scholars and schools in Asia, Europe and South America, with Africa coming along, are following the dominant research paradigm because of the focus on a common set of "top" journals. International scholars adapt their research approach to meet the expectations and preferences of the "A-journal" editors and reviewers.

By choosing the most popular topics and using the most prevalent theories and methods, papers are looking more and more alike with fewer and fewer new ideas.

Is it socially responsible scholarship to write papers solely to get them published without regard to their intellectual and social value? It is no overstatement to say that our research enterprise is at risk. By disconnecting from the world of practical management, engaging in questionable research practices, focusing on career needs and pursuing high rankings, scholarship is largely socially *irresponsible*. It is failing to meet the goal of science: to discover truth and improve the human condition.

How long will taxpayers, private and public funding agencies, and society at large tolerate these self-serving, inward-looking, "castle in the sky" research practices?

The good news is that these criticisms and discontent are beginning to motivate actions.

Scholars are recognising that we should reconsider how we evaluate research quality and impact. Many admit that citations in academic journals do not necessarily indicate practical, social and perhaps even intellectual impact.

On December 16, 2012, 155 editors and publishers of scholarly journals in a variety of disciplines representing 82 organisations worldwide gathered in San Francisco to sign a declaration along with specific suggestions for a new framework for assessing research contribution.

They declared: Do not use journal-based metrics, such as Journal Impact Factors, as a surrogate measure of the quality of individual research articles to assess an individual scientist's contributions or in hiring, promotion or funding decisions.

An article in the Sept/Oct 2014 issue of *BizEd* discussed the topic of "Measuring faculty impact", advocating a broadened metric that includes books, chapters, professional services, media coverage and expert witness appearances. In 2013

82

On December 16, 2012, 155 editors and publishers of scholarly journals representing 82 organisations gathered to sign a declaration for assessing research contribution

20%

Analyses of articles in leading management journals reveal that 80% of published research focuses on economic outcomes. Much less research, only 20%, focuses on social outcomes such as stress, health, satisfaction, justice, social responsibility and environmental stewardship

80%

Workplace stress in the US causes major human havoc: studies have shown that between 40% and 80% of employees experience stress at work and about 50% have symptoms of burnout

AACSB revised its standards for accreditation to include sustainability and impact. All business schools will be assessed using the new standards by 2016.

EFMD's EQUIS accreditation system considers contribution to world sustainability as a criterion in assessing teaching and research quality. The Research Excellence Framework in UK revised its assessment of institutional research quality by putting a 25% weighting on social or practical impact. Similar efforts are being introduced in Australia, the Netherlands and France. Those are important steps toward socially responsible scholarship.

Analysis of articles in leading management journals reveal that 80% of published research focuses on economic outcomes such as firm performance, productivity, market value, innovation or efficiency. Much less research, only 20%, focuses on social outcomes such as stress, health, satisfaction, justice, social responsibility and environmental stewardship.

We spend much of our time and funds helping firms gain profits without concern about possible harmful consequences to other stakeholders and the world at large.

Socially responsible scholarship should aim to understand how firms could be people-friendly and planet-friendly. An example of an important people-friendly topic is work stress.

Workplace stress in the US causes major human havoc: studies have shown that between 40% and 80% of employees experience stress at work and about 50% have symptoms of burnout. Stress-related expenses such as accidents, absenteeism, and mental or physical health problems cost the US about $300 billion in 2012, not including intangible costs to employees in terms of lost mental wellbeing, happiness and longevity.

Socially responsible research should identify the major work stressors and test management policies and practices that can reduce stress.

Studies can compare planet-friendly and unfriendly practices in organisations. It can study how firms can be profitable without depleting the earth's natural resources and without damaging our environment. It can strive to develop a new model of business that holds firms accountable for the natural resources used and damaged, and for the damage done to the environment during production processes. Changing the focus of research from benefiting the firm or shareholders primarily to a balanced focus on benefiting all stakeholders is another important step toward socially responsible scholarship.

"

Socially responsible scholarship means that we think about how our research can benefit our research participants and beneficiaries as much as it benefits ourselves. It means that we treat research participants with gratitude and respect

Socially responsible scholarship means that we think about how our research can benefit our research participants and beneficiaries as much as it benefits ourselves. It means that we treat research participants with gratitude and respect.

Why should managers and employees support business school research that is irrelevant to them? Why should they participate in studies that are undertaken to produce papers that meet researchers' or schools' needs but not theirs?

Why should granting agencies support research that gives researchers promotions and employment security but makes no contribution to society through important discoveries or inventions? What entitles researchers to use public goods for their private gains? Considering these value proposition questions is an important part of socially responsible scholarship.

Who should take responsibility for ensuring that business school research fulfils the social mission of contributing valid and useful knowledge?

In my conversations with faculty and school leadership, everyone passes the buck. Faculty researchers point to the school leadership or deans. Deans point to the university administration or the senior faculty on tenure and promotion committees. University administrators point to the government research grant and assessment bodies.

However, as Gandhi said: "be the change you want to see in the world". We should all take responsibility to solve this problem and save our research enterprise.

Randy Schekman, recipient of the 2013 Nobel Prize in physiology and medicine, is one who has taken a personal initiative. Recognising that journals encourage researchers to pursue fashionable topics, distort the scientific process and encourage short-cuts, he declared the day before he received the Nobel Prize that he will no longer submit papers to *Nature, Cell* and *Science*, the three top science journals.

Researchers can collectively change journal policies and practices. As some editors have said, "journals can only publish papers submitted." Scholars and journal editors (who themselves are important scholars) can bring about a shift from writing journal-focused papers to knowledge-generation and practice-improvement scholarship. They can change research from controlled paper production to a sacred journey of scientific inquiry. That is the spirit of socially responsible scholarship.

The most important beneficiaries of research – business leaders – are also the most distant from and dispassionate about business school research. Although they have been largely passive recipients, they could have tremendous power if they become active consumers demanding relevant research.

Academic–practitioner collaboration could be a win-win proposition. Business leaders could influence research by providing funding and offering their companies as research laboratories. Practitioners' interests, understandably, are aligned more with the traditional emphasis on economic than the much-needed social outcomes. To ensure balanced attention to social outcomes, funding agencies should devote more of their research dollars to addressing social outcomes affected by organisational policies and practices.

All parties in the research enterprise – scholars, school leaders, grant agencies, policymakers, business leaders and journal editors – can contribute to the pursuit of socially responsible scholarship by remembering the goal of science: the discovery and application of true knowledge to improve the human condition.

FURTHER INFORMATION

References to original work mentioned in this article are available from the author – anne.tsui@asu.edu

ABOUT THE AUTHOR

Professor Anne S Tsui is the Visiting Distinguished Professor at the Mendoza College of Business, University of Notre Dame, in the US. She is also Distinguished Professor at Peking University, Fudan University and Shanghai Jiao Tong University, all in China, and Emeritus Professor of International Management, Arizona State University. She has served as the 67th President of the Academy of Management and Founding President of the International Association for Chinese Management Research. She is the 14th Editor of the Academy of Management Journal and Founding Editor-in-Chief of Management and Organization Review, a journal dedicated to research about China and emerging economies.

Section_03
Rigour-Relevance and Business School Impact

"A new wave of social pressures and requests is infusing the higher-education 'milieu'. Around the world, societies are demanding a real social engagement from higher-education institutions"

Paul Beaulieu
'Intentional Impact from Business Schools'

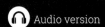 Audio version

Volume   Issue

13_03

Flexible
future

2019

Intentional Impact from Business Schools

Paul Beaulieu explains how, in response to a new wave of social demands, business schools should adopt a more comprehensive and responsible social engagement. This may pave the way for the emergence of a new generation of business schools

A new wave of social pressures and requests is infusing the higher-education *milieu*. Around the world, societies are demanding a real social engagement from higher-education institutions. Inside most of societies around the world, key-stakeholders that are related to the future of higher education ask for a strategic realignment and active engagement of the HE's institutions. Business schools represent a very large part of every national higher education systems. These social requests for real impacts on societal advancement pave the way for an improvement of the social legitimacy of business schools. This new wave of social pressures becomes manifest through the HE's governance mechanisms, especially national councils for research, ministries responsible for higher education, and/or advisory councils composed of business school stakeholders.

This new upspring of interest in the development of social engagement and active participation in societal change resonates particularly inside business schools. In tandem with other evolving economic and societal developments, the debate concerning the roles and the specific missions of business schools has taken many turns during the course of the last two decades with the most critical juncture for this debate undoubtedly being the shockwave of the 2008 global financial crisis and a certain feeling of culpability it imposed within business school establishments, particularly in the US.

Beyond the traditional

The business schools sector is highly diversified in term of offer and context and these social demands aim for an active re-focusing of the mission of business schools into societal transformation. It also seeks an improved contribution in the field of the management of all types of enterprises. These desired changes go beyond the traditional provision of market-driven professional competencies and the traditional role of providing research findings to scientific

This new upspring of interest in the development of social engagement and active participation in societal change resonates particularly inside business schools

research communities. Societies now want true intentional societal impact (ie purposeful change effects) and performance-based strategies for bringing about transformative evolution of social changes.

The business schools are clearly effective in managing and implementing the three traditional lines of business they have institutionalised: professional education and executive training; scientific research and publishing; and internal and external community participation.

But many still have difficulties in integrating and leveraging the results of these three elements. State governance bodies and financial mechanisms that provide oversight and funding for the higher education sector have already introduced accountability and impact norms that have generally been limited to proxy-indicators of performance; moreover, these have not been designed to measure real social transformations.

Much of the evaluation done by these institutions are more focused on the "compliance" end of the accountability continuum rather than the impact end; this has led to focuses on efficiency and effectiveness rather than impact and relevance.

The socio-political requests directed to business schools for targeted societal contributions and impacts are more involved and thought-out in terms of scope. They are also much more embedded in the social needs for transformative-capabilities development than they used to be.

These new capabilities are urgently required given the context of increasing scaling-up of global complexity due to major structuring effects generated through multidimensional and multinational challenges such as climate change, social inequalities, global population explosion, natural resources depletion, social exasperation about business social responsibilities and so on.

There is now an emerging consensus on the agenda's priority: business schools of all organisational configurations must care proactively for the future of humanity and for the societies they exist to serve.

Advocacy statements for societal impact

The call for a collective approach to generating expected impacts on society comes from all levels and domains of the higher-education and business school sector, including their key-stakeholders.

This call for a significant change in the nature and priority afforded to social engagement within these business schools goes much further than promotion or accountability related to its economic footprint (local and national) or its usual contributions to the myriad self-sustained scientific communities enclosed in the scientific field and distanced from management practice.

The following advocacy statements and propositions coming from key institutional stakeholders of the sector are representative and worth noting as "translators" of the scope of the desired change required from business schools:

The Academy of Management's (AOM) theme for its 2010 annual conference (*Dare to Care*) and most of its presidential addresses that followed voiced the necessity for collective action and responsible engagement and for the scholarly community to be more outwardly looking and involved in relevant social problems. The AOM formalised this intent in its key strategic objective statement for 2022: "Advancing the impact of management and organisation science on business and society worldwide".

The global initiative launched by the *Community for Responsible Research in Business and Management* and its manifesto *Horizon 2030* is explicitly "a call ... to action for directing research toward achieving humanity's highest aspirations".

The proposed change for the role of business school research is significant: responsible research for the advancement of humanity instead of a limited focus on the agent capabilities (individual managers or corporations).

In Europe, 20 years after the Bologna Declaration the *European Higher Education Area* is moving the strategic institutional focus of development from structural changes to fundamental values essential to the contribution of higher education to society.

In congruence with the *Magna Charta Universitatum* promulgated in 1988, the *Global Forum on Academic Freedom, Institutional Autonomy and Future of Democracy* held in June 2019 at the Council of Europe in Strasbourg reiterated what it recognised as the imperative core value of higher education: the freedom of intervention by academics and their institutions for the advancement of societies and the effectiveness of their social engagement.

Scholarship with impact is a recurrent thematic of the strategic conversation inside the scientific communities and managerial forums within the sector. Lead-scholars such as Andrew Pettigrew, Howard Thomas, Arnoud De Meyer, Peter McKiernan, Denise Rousseau, Jeffrey Pfeffer, Henry Mintzberg, Michel Kalika and Eric Cornuel (among many others) repeatedly argued the "unfulfilled promises" of management education and proposed new roles that should be performed by business schools in society.

2022

The AOM formalised its key strategic objective statement for 2022: Advancing the impact of management and organisation science on business and society worldwide

Recurrent debates are ignited on this topic, leading many to posit that there is a shared apprehension that business schools and/or management studies have "lost their way". In fact, this is seen as a translation into an acute institutional sense of erosion in legitimacy and social recognition.

The *social impact of research* is becoming another clear priority for state governing bodies and their dedicated agencies responsible for higher education, science and innovation policies. In 2022 the final report of the European Research Area Board of the European Commission called for a *New Renaissance for Innovating Europe out of the Crisis*"in the sense of an "Innovation Union" for the advancement of societies.

The recent *Impact Pathways Guidelines* for mission-oriented research in Europe is again another explicit call for a more transformation-driven social sciences agenda in which business schools play an important role.

Since Ernest Boyer's report (1990) for the Carnegie Foundation, the definition and the implementation of a diversity of types of legitimate scholarship is becoming an expanding reality. The movement for engaged-scholarship with society's needs gained in recognition and penetration through academic practices.

In the business school sector we have seen the call for change coming from eminent scholars such as James March in the *Scholar's Quest*, Donald Schön on the legitimacy of *Knowing-in-Action*, Andrew Van De Ven on *Engaged Scholarship* in organisational research and Denise Rousseau through the development of the international network dedicated to the development of *Evidence-Based Management* for the advancement of management practice effectiveness.

The *knowledge and scholarly communication* field and its processes are also engaged in a profound cycle of transformation and evolutionary changes. Open-edition is in progressive implementation and all kinds of stakeholders are asking for a better access to knowledge. This is significantly contributing to a call for academic communities and institutions to better communicate the results of their investigations to society and not just into relatively "closed" scientific communities of peers.

The existential challenges that faces the printed media dedicated to knowledge opens a strategic learning opportunity for business schools to begin to transfer "disintermediated-knowledge" directly to communities of practice and to society generally.

Finally, *practice-turn* began to challenge the traditional academic isolation of scholarly contributions in the field of business. It has done this by raising the awareness of a specific area of knowledge's logic and epistemology in both communities of practice and the real-life networks of context-based practices.

Front-runner in this direction are current initiatives dedicated to professional domains that define and frame doctoral studies and qualifications alongside a practice-based research epistemology and a practice-knowledge ecology.

In summary, the interest in the social impact of business schools and their activities is not new. This is an organic process and it will take time, experimentation and confrontation to mature into explicit and grounded formal appeals addressed to business schools.

But in the meantime, some of these schools will proactively realign their mission to address this new agenda of social contribution and intentional impact. Progressively we may observe the emergence of a new generation of business schools, strategically oriented to a new realisation of their institutional mission articulated on the intentional achievement of an "orchestrated portfolio" of actions geared toward desired societal impacts.

This means that those institutions will have to become "outwardly-centred" and more integrated to society, including to contextualised management practice.

This also requires a certain detachment from the traditional strategic paradigm of

mechanical market relations limited to traditional programme outputs (learning and/or research) as compared to intentional outcomes and social changes contributions.

Capabilities for social impact

As noted above, the intentional generation of societal impacts will require new capabilities of business schools and the development of a rigorous practice of strategic impact management.

The actual state of the conversation related to impact still needs to evolve. It will need to go through a series of basic development steps to gain in maturity and align on current best practice related to outcomes and contribution management and evaluation.

Briefly, the four "cornerstones", that could contribute to the implementation of a reliable social impact management practice are:

This means that those institutions will have to become "outwardly-centred" and more integrated to society, including to contextualised management practice

• Improvement and clarification of the key concepts and the *framework of common understanding* as well as the methodologies related to intentional outcomes and impact management and evaluation. Outputs of existing programmes are not what we recognise as systemic and purposeful impacts within society.

Social impact related to mid-term and long-term social changes is clearly in the upstream of programme outputs. Social impacts refer to structuring-effects and changes induced into societal systems for social improvement.

Impact management is definitively a complex function and, for those who must succeed at it, a demanding field of practice. Existing experience, knowledge and methodologies of contribution and outcome analysis, programme-based theories of change management and utilisation-focused or principle-focused evaluation are already developed and practised in fields such as social intervention, development studies and evaluation sciences.

• Business schools will need to develop and implement *impact management processes, strategies and systems*. The EFMD-BSIS initiative "Business School Impact System" recognises and supports the implementation of an impact evaluation process. Even if in reality a large part of organisational

strategies is emergent, it will be good management practice to plan and formulate intentional impact strategies in partnership with key business school stakeholders.

• To accelerate the learning-curve of impact management we should actively encourage the *development of communities of research and practice* related to business schools' social impact. The AACSB and the EFMD are already performing a series of periodical activities focused on the sharing of experience in relation to impact of business schools. It should be complemented by a global community of research, strongly practice-oriented, that would be dedicated to impact management in the field of business.

• Sooner or later it will be appropriate to have some mechanisms and standards for the accreditation of the organisational processes and systems specific to the generation of impact claims. It will become a relative necessity in order to assure the validity, reliability and fidelity of the *quality of the impact's claims* publicised by diverse business schools.

Standards for information presentation, as we have seen from the *Global Reporting Initiative* in the field of corporate sustainable responsibility could be an example of the kind of standards developed for impact information. Strategic intentional social-impact management will definitively be an opportunity for business schools to differentiate themselves and their contributions to society. It will evidently become a development path and a proofing practice of responsible social engagement.

About the Author

Professor Paul Beaulieu is Professor at the School of Management Sciences of the University of Quebec in Montreal, Canada. His domain of expertise is related to the institutional development and management of higher-education institutions

Section_04
Uncertain Futures and Transformational Change

"It seems beyond doubt that the schools are going to be hit by a disruptive innovation from the new online courses. In my terms, the intruders will steal a march on the incumbents and get to the second curve ahead of them. Change so often comes by the bypass, unnoticed until it is right there, already ahead of you"

Charles Handy
'The past is not the future'

 Audio version

Volume   Issue

09_03

2015

The past is not the future

Business schools – and the businesses they serve – need to discover a "second curve" if they are to survive and prosper. By **Charles Handy**

When I last spoke to the EFMD conference in 1974 my talk reflected my own personal dilemma. I was at the time the Director of the MBA Programme at the London Business School (although it was then technically still called an MSc because London University did not recognise the MBA as a graduate degree).

I found myself presiding over a programme that I could not fully believe in but was unable to change.

I had soon realised that there are limits to how much you can teach about the practice of management in a classroom. I, along with all my colleagues, had gone through American business schools and had adopted their classroom-based models as the prototypes for ours.

For some reason we did not look to our own examples of other professional schools – architecture, law, medicine or accounting – all of which combined classroom instruction with a form of tutored apprenticeship. It became clear to me then that the MBA more accurately stood for Master of Business Analysis.

There is nothing wrong in that so far as it goes. The problem was that it did not go far enough. We were, in effect, training consultants not managers. And as future consultants, the best of our students were rapidly picked up by consulting firms and investment banks. That was not, I felt, what we were there for.

We also followed the American model along with the Ford and Carnegie Reports and anchored our school in the University of London. I had naively though that this would allow me to import occasional teachers from their faculties, such as those of philosophy, law and political theory as well as history and science, because I believed that business analysis needed to be enriched by other disciplines to provide a more rounded preparation for a management role.

I soon discovered, however, that the traditional faculties of the university regarded us as a cuckoo in their nest and wanted nothing to do with us. Nor did my own colleagues welcome the thoughts of any such intrusions. What we did import, alas, was the university ethos, one that valued published research more than teaching ability for career promotion. The result was a school that was effectively a collection of subject silos and colleagues who were pushed to teach subjects rather than students.

One of the problems was that almost all of my colleagues were pure academics. They had never had to put their knowledge to work in businesses or any other organisation.

But knowing *What* does not automatically guarantee knowing *How*, let alone knowing *Why*.

In desperation I found myself running workshops in communication skills and listening exercises. But these were inadequate sops in what I saw as a wrongly focused system. I worried that we were turning loose clever but unskilled graduates into a world that desperately needed effective leaders and managers.

The development of our future managers was effectively delegated to myself as programme director. It was in recognition of this that I was promoted to Professor of Management Development, one of only two such titles in Britain, or in Europe, at the time.

It was probably in recognition of my rarity value that I was asked to be one of the early Trustees of the newly formed EFMD, which, indeed, became my sanctuary and haven in those years. It would be interesting to know how many Professors of Management Development there are in this hall today. Few, if any, I suspect. That, I fear, is a symptom of one of our problems – the main purpose of our existence is not recognised academically or culturally.

Even the research that became the focus of attention of most of my colleagues was not the ground-breaking stuff of the physical sciences but rather a recording and interpretation of what was happening in the real laboratories of management, the businesses themselves. Again, useful but not future shaping.

In general, we followed our customers, those same businesses, serving their wishes and using the best of them as our models. We seldom wanted to challenge them, content to feed them with new entrants groomed to their ways.

It was a strategy that made us a successful business but not, I felt, a transformative educational institution. I remember well the day when a journalist rang me to enquire what LBS thought of a new government initiative aimed at business. I heard myself saying "The school does not think...." before stopping myself and suggesting she talk to a particular member of the faculty.

Then I reflected, should not the school have a view on current events? All that brainpower going to waste because we were a collection of individuals not a group with a view. In my more cynical moments I reflected that I was more truthfully the curator of an elite pond where the businesses came to fish for talent and the students came to be hooked.

As long as my recruitment process captured the right sort of fish everyone was happy, irrespective of what we taught them or what they learned. Anecdotally, past students would tell me that they had enjoyed a tough and stimulating educational experience, one that had made them more self-confident and had led onto a good job, but that they had so far found little use of anything particular that they had learned.

Indeed the surveys, then as now, indicated that only 10% of our learning came from books or study. No wonder, perhaps, that I was disconsolate.

That was more than 40 years ago. Since those pioneering days when business schools were hardly known outside the US they have multiplied around the world.

There are now thought to be over 10,000 business schools overall with nearly 5,000 in India alone. The MBA is a global brand, with many young people seeing it as the necessary entry ticket to good jobs and big salaries.

Clearly my misgivings did not worry anyone else. It is a great success story. But success can lead to wilful blindness and the belief that all will continue as it has in the past. Are they right or are they unwittingly on the road to Davy's Bar?

"Davy's Bar" alludes to something that happened to me some years ago and has subsequently led to my own "Theory of Everything".

One day I was driving through the Wicklow Mountains behind Dublin when I found myself uncertain about the right road to take. I saw a man by the roadside so I asked him if I was on the right road to Avoca.

x10

Costs are soaring, in research as well as teaching, with the average two-year programme costing $120,000, ten times the cost of one online

15yrs

Richard Lyons estimates that half of US business schools will be out of business in less than 10 years. Clayton Christensen reckons that half of the American universities will be bankrupt in 15 years

10%

Indeed the surveys, then as now, indicated that only 10% of our learning came from books or study.

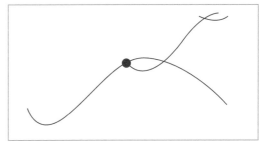

"❞

The second curve has to start before the first curve peaks because otherwise there are no resources or energy to cover the early investment that will start the second curve

'You are indeed," he said, "and it's easy, just go on up the hill for two or three kilometres, then down for a while until you cross a small bridge and see Davy's Bar on the other side. You can't miss it, it is bright red. Have you got that?"

"Yes. I think so," I said.

"Well, half a kilometre before you get there turn right up the hill."

It sounded so clear that I drove off before I realised what he had said. I got to the bar, turned round and found the right road but as I drove on I thought that in life we cannot do that, miss the road and turn back.

Too many businesses that I knew have ended up in Davy's Bar having missed the turn to the future and can only reminisce about the good times and how they missed their opportunity to change direction.

I went on to formulate my experience as a general principle, the "Law of the Sigmoid Curve", the curve of everything human or made by humans, businesses, governments even empires and, of course, our own lives.

Any and everything will start with an investment of some sort, be it money, ideas or education. More goes out than comes in for a time. Then the line picks up and grows and grows until, eventually, it peaks and thereafter starts to decline. The eventual decline is inevitable; all we can do is determine how long the line might be and at what place we are on it.

That is a depressing prospect for the human race but there is an escape from the inevitable. We can start a second and even a third curve:

The trouble is that the second curve has to start before the first curve peaks because otherwise there are no resources or energy to cover the early investment that will start the second curve. Obvious that may be, but it is hugely difficult in practice because the need to start second curve thinking comes just when everything is going well, when all the implicit messages urge one to continue the status quo.

Where are the business schools on that first curve now? Some believe that they are nowhere near the peak of the curve. LBS has recently raised £100 million to buy and refit the nearby City Hall with a suite of new lecture theatres, confident that life will go on as before only more so.

On the other side of the ocean Richard Lyons of Berkeley's Hass School estimates that one-half of US business schools will be out of business in less than 10 years. Clayton Christensen of Harvard reckons that half of the American universities will be bankrupt in 15 years. Part-time participants and GMAT applications are both declining.

Meanwhile, costs are soaring, in research as well as teaching, with the average two-year programme costing $120,000, ten times the cost of one online.

Roger Martin, former dean of the Rotman School of Management at the University of Toronto in Canada, has calculated that the total cost of one published article is now $400,000 and something like $1.7 million for one that is actually used by managers.

Are business schools becoming just too expensive to survive as they are today? It is my sense, from perusing the excellent publications by Howard Thomas and others on the Future of Management Education for the EFMD, that most of the business schools of the world are at or maybe even beyond the peak in the curve.

It seems beyond doubt that the schools are going to be hit by a disruptive innovation from the new online courses. In my terms, the intruders will steal a march on the incumbents and get to the second curve ahead of them. Change so often comes by the bypass, unnoticed until it is right there, already ahead of you.

The paradox is that just when business schools may be beginning to hit the buffers they will actually be needed more than ever. Businesses are getting ever more complex, too big to be human scale and too self-absorbed to be seen as legitimate to wider society.

These businesses also need to find a second curve, one that defines a new purpose, new structures and new values and therefore requires a new sort of leadership. The opportunity is there for the business schools to match their second curves to those of the corporation, but are they up to the challenge?

They probably have five to 10 years to find that new curve while current programmes keep them going – that is the point of the overlap in the curves, it gives time for experiment. PepsiCo, I understand, does this routinely, with two groups in each division, one promoting the current strategy, the other seeking to disrupt it before others do.

So what should be the elements of that second curve? You are, of course, better placed than me to answer that. But as a concerned outsider I might be allowed to express a view. I have a rule of thumb that if a computer or the internet can do what you do, then let them do it and move onto things that they cannot do. In this case this means leaving a lot of the *What* syllabus to online courses and concentrating on the *How* and the *Why*.

Essentially that means concentrating on manager development rather than management education – a subtle but crucial change of words. It means moving away from the university and towards the work organisation.

"

Concentrating on manager development rather than management education – a subtle but crucial change of words – means moving away from the university and towards the work organisation

Different faculty will often be needed, often drawn from outside, and different faculty reward systems will be needed. Maybe the business schools should become leadership academies to recognise the change in emphasis.

Second, in place of research that records/interprets current practice, the new academies should turn themselves into think tanks, exploring the future – of business, of capitalism, of organisation structures and the role of regulation and so on.

These are big asks, which require big changes but my fear is that, left to continue as they are, the schools will become shadows of their former selves, slimmed down, with shorter, cheaper courses, poorer faculty and shabby buildings, relics abandoned in the sands of time.

This article is an edited transcript of an address by Professor Charles Handy to the EFMD Annual Conference, June 2015, in Brussels.

Bestselling author
of *The Empty Raincoat*

Charles Handy

THE
SECOND
CURVE

Thoughts On
Reinventing Society

Above

In *The Second Curve*, Handy builds on a life's work to glimpse into the future and what challenges and opportunities lie ahead. Provacative and thoughtful as ever, he sets out the questions we all need to ask ourselves – and points us in the direction of some of the answers.

The Second Curve, is published by Penguin Random House and available in print and e version from Amazon.co.uk

gf

Section_04
Uncertain Futures and Transformational Change

"Business education and the business schools need to be re-imagined, adapted to and help shape the (a brighter) future. Business as usual is bad business"

Christopher Pitelis
'A future for business education:
why business as usual is bad business'

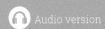 Audio version

Volume   Issue

13_02

2019

A future for business education: why business as usual is bad business

Chris Pitelis calls for a re-imagining of business education and business schools so they can help build a better and brighter future

Business schools themselves kept improving in numerous ways and gaining academic credibility, often drawing on their disciplinary foundations

Business education is relatively young, about 140 years old. It started as a case study-based approach with little by way of a conceptual foundations. Nevertheless, it has become very successful. Circa one in five students in the US are enrolled in a business education programme.

Over time, there emerged prestigious specialised conferences, journals, accreditors and other bodies and metrics that have helped foster a diverse and seemingly robust ecosystem.

Things were not always so good. The author studied economics in the UK and recalls the disdain with which business faculty and studies on "the floor below" were regarded by economists - as little more than glorified consultants.

In some ways that was deserved. Emerging business and management schools would normally tend to attract the scholars who could not succeed in their field by being too applied and/or too heterodox and/or simply not good. Few fields, such as marketing and accounting partly escaped the stigma of being compared to scholars and departments of a founding discipline; others such as international business aimed to be multidisciplinary to start with, partly escaping the founding discipline "curse", yet struggled to convince the wider academic community of its rigour and sometimes even its *raison d'etre*.

In this context the subsequent success of business schools was neither self-evident nor, to my knowledge, has it been adequately understood and explained. There are a few possible related reasons.

A key reason in my view is that business education has gradually served as a "general purpose technology" (GPT). GPTs, such as the internet, are technologies/innovations that have multiple applications and are scalable (consider

Google algorithms). Business education - imparted knowledge shares in part, these characteristics.

Business schools themselves kept improving in numerous ways and gaining academic credibility, often drawing on their disciplinary foundations of economics, sociology, psychology and quantitative methods while increasingly aiming to adapt to business reality and develop and improve new theories for their own purposes.

The need for and pursuit of scholarly legitimacy also drove the emergence of "elite" journals with demanding conceptual and methodological rigour. Books, meanwhile, have been delegated to practitioners and hobbyists.

As in other subjects, notably economics, the focus on "research" gradually gave rise to diminishing returns. The pressures for publication in elite journals with the almost excessive reward in terms of promotion, tenure and overall gravitas has raised concerns about the potential trade-off between research, teaching, leadership and engagement. Many a top publication is seen as largely irrelevant to real-life business and practitioners.

While a number of top schools had the resources to hire individuals who could excel in elite and relevant research (as well as on teaching and leadership) usually with supporting structures and business models and procedures, not everyone could follow. And the impact on life-work balance gradually started become excessive.

Students paying high fees began questioning the relevance of top-tier research to their learning experience. Similarly, many businesses and business people questioned the relevance and usefulness of business degrees. All this led to calls for change with a gradual re-balancing and more focus on engagement, impact and teaching.

1 in 5

Circa one in five students in the US are enrolled in a business education programme

It could be argued that the evolution of business education has gone from practice to theory and back to practice. I think, however, that the reality is more nuanced than that. What we see is a re-emergent focus on teaching, engagement, relevance and impact, taking place from stronger conceptual foundations -- that of "engaged scholarship"-- that could be imparted to and co-developed with the student body and other stakeholders.

The return to practice in the form of engaged scholarship is, in this sense, at a higher plane than before. It has been co-constituted through public policy innovations such as the REF (Research Excellence Framework) and the T(eaching) EF and now the K(nowledge) EF in the UK as well as the role of business school dean associations such as CABS (UK) and ABDC (Australia) and accreditation bodies such as the EFMD, AACSB and AMBA providing rules and metrics to measure and improve sustainable performance.

Today business education is a multi-billion-euro sector. But it is also looking rather tired and ill-adapted to today's realities. MBA numbers are declining in many countries and the cost-benefit calculus of business degrees is under question. Popular magazines, such as Fortune, wonder what is killing business education in the US.

Factors such as immigration and neo-protectionist policies by governments contribute. And so does increasing supply and competition from numerous sources including new national markets and alternative providers. All these are widely acknowledged and discussed. The question whether competition harms or helps expand the market remains an open one.

Here I wish to focus on some aspects that can benefit from more attention. These relate to the student experience, the role of business in the global financial crisis, the 4th industrial revolution and the rise of big tech.

Starting with students, the success of business education led to business schools often becoming the cash cows of financially challenged institutions. Gradually this has led to lop-sided (as compared to other schools and departments) staff-student-ratios (SSRs), unhealthy life-work balance and high salaries.

"

Dealing with social and economic sustainability requires a focus on ethics and morality

At the same time, increasing fees and even a rather self-defeating approach by some institutions to treat students as "customers", have led to those customers demanding value for money and sometimes expecting to "buy" what they paid for (a good degree) one way or the other. Combine this with increasing demands on academics for research output as opposed to teaching excellence and things gradually came to a head.

During the years of "irrational exuberance" business scholars like many economists, have gradually come to believe in the self-correcting properties of markets and the ability of business to help address societal problems. That led to a suspicion of public policy and a sharp decline in the perceived need for government involvement in terms of antitrust action, regulation, competition and other policies.

The focus on business has also been prejudicial on engagement with the "third sector". That has helped undermine economic sustainability and in many ways business education became complicit on practices that helped bring about the global financial crisis.

It was not rare for business school cases to heap praise on the acumen and practices of businesses that were later involved in the major scandals; consider Enron and Theranos.

In the meantime, the failure to seriously consider antitrust legislation helped the currently dominant tech monopolies, a concurrent worsening in income distribution, little regard for the environment and basically an institutional failure of unprecedented dimension.

Not surprisingly, many a commentator, including numerous documentaries and dramatisations of the crisis, questioned the role and legitimacy of business education. With business schools depending more than others on business engagement, executive education/consulting and business-related research, and the emergent conflict of interest is not too hard to see. It is hard to be critical of your funder even at the most basic personal level.

Increasingly that led to demands for more arm's length engagement and the inclusion of ethics, governance and sustainability–related issues in the business curriculum. Yet its is clear that this follows than leads. Different pressures emerged from the 4th industrial revolution. This includes developments such as artificial intelligence, robotics, 3D printing, blockchain, internet of things, self-driving and electric vehicles, smart cities and so on. None of those plays to the current provision of business education. They are simply too science and engineering based for the current business model of business schools.

Business education needs to adapt and to lead. For this it needs to enhance its provision with subjects that are able to address the key challenges cited above and others. Dealing with social and economic sustainability requires a focus on ethics and morality --this can come from philosophy. The influence of philosophy and epistemology on business has so far been minimal.

Antitrust action requires incorporating law. Law and economics have found applications in the corporate governance debate but here, too, business scholars mostly followed the economists' emphasis on shareholder value.

Things are changing, but slowly. Incorporating law into the curriculum can help. The same applies to politics. The current power of big tech is much more than market power -- it has morphed into political power. It is important that power becomes a major subject in business curricula -- hence politics and geo-politics as well.

The above has focused on social sciences. The 4th industrial revolution calls for expanding the curriculum to science and engineering. Business schools need to do with relevant science subjects what they before achieved with (selected) social sciences.

If all the above sounds a bit like "business education imperialism" and a very tall order indeed, it is because it is. It cannot be readily achieved by individual schools, even the most resourced and resourceful ones. It requires collaboration, intra and inter-university, close and arm's length collaboration, and partnerships with business but also with the public sector, with the polity (the third sector) and with all key constituents of the supporting ecosystem, such as accreditors.

It also requires discipline-based interdisciplinary. Despite praise heaped on multi and interdisciplinary behaviour, the reality on the ground remains that these are not rewarded, incentivised or facilitated. They are very few if any inter-disciplinary journals, conferences and accreditation bodies.

Arguably, inter-disciplinarily works best when each participant is an expert in his or her discipline and learns from each other -- not when everyone is a jack-of-all trades and knows a little about everything. While there is need for the rare neo-renaissance multi-expert individual and for "communication facilitators", more often than not reality and expanding knowledge calls for specialisation, division of labour and co-operation.

It is unlikely that the above can be effected with the same modalities as before. For one, the scale may be prohibiting to all but the very few. This requires genuine intra- and inter-university

partnerships and deep thinking about what makes good for purpose structures and business models. It also requires accreditors adapting to the new reality. And it requires business education itself not committing euthanasia by undermining the development of the very subject matters on which its continuing sustainable success depends.

The closures of liberal arts, philosophy, economics and sociology departments on financial grounds kills the goose that lays the golden egg. Business educators should be prepared and willing to keep subsidising the subjects that helped them succeed .

I will close with a call to bring back the good old book. In my area (strategic international business and organisation) virtually most key ideas emanated from a handful of classic books on economics by Joe Bain, Edith Penrose, Cyert and March, Nelson and Winter, Oliver Williamson and Stephen Hymer.

In part this is because exploring adequately a single overarching and fungible argument and its implications requires space, time-frame and method that are poorly aligned to elite journal publications. With few exceptions, such as the resource and capabilities based view, the record of management scholars in coming up with new theory is lamentable. There are, for sure, very many good ideas and advances but no new overarching general theories like those proposed by the aforementioned economics scholars. Here again we are followers.

Bringing the book back in, developing our own theories and methods can help end this dependence on fields such as economics that are increasingly becoming irrelevant yet paradoxically the dominant source of theory. We can and should do better.

Business education and the business schools need to be re-imagined, adapted to and help shape the (a brighter) future. Business as usual is bad business. It is hoped that this article may help by inviting a debate.

About the Author

Professor Christos Pitelis is Dean of the College of Business, Abu Dhabi University

Section_04
Uncertain Futures and Transformational Change

"Thanks to technology, education will not just be about acquiring the knowledge needed to do this or that job. Rather, it will allow us to help develop a student's personality by focusing particularly on their strengths, adapting the time spent studying to their needs and capacity"

Santiago Iniguez
'The future is blended'

🎧 Audio version

Volume   Issue

11_01

2016

The future is blended

Santiago Iniguez explains why business schools and corporations must accommodate the increasing role of technology in education

There is a fear, expressed frequently, that technology will replace professors. But I can say emphatically and unequivocally, THAT IT WILL NOT SUBSTITUTE THEM.

Bill Gates
Road to the Future, 1995;
capital letters in the original

The question is not whether I can invest big, it is whether I can learn fast.

C K Prahalad
World Innovation Forum, 2009

Technology, in parallel with developments in cognitive psychology and education sciences, is producing a formidable paradigm shift in the learning process and the mission of educators and, of course, in business schools.

Traditionally, the objective of education has been standardisation: to teach students the "three Rs", prepare them for a particular job, and help them develop the skills required to engage in and contribute to society.

That said, the future of the learning process is focused on personalised development, seen as an opportunity to stretch and strengthen each individual's qualities. This is where the real change lies.

Thanks to technology, education will not just be about acquiring the knowledge needed to do this or that job. Rather, it will allow us to help develop a student's personality by focusing particularly on their strengths, adapting the time spent studying to their needs and capacity – all while measuring the results of the learning process and which teaching methods best help with personal and professional development. This personalisation will undoubtedly foster the entrepreneurial profile of learners and identify many new job opportunities.

Though it may sound counterintuitive, technology can humanise the learning process. We sometimes look at technology as an obstacle to personalisation, proximity, sociability and humanity but this fallacy is rooted in the myth that technology is a threat to mankind – for example, the destruction of jobs through automation and, in short, that the robots will end up taking over the world.

Aside from adapting to learners' circumstances, the integration of technology and teaching brings teachers closer to their students and students closer to one another. It also helps teachers with repetitive tasks such as assessing academic performance, passing on basic information and answering frequently asked questions.

In doing so, technology frees teachers' time, allowing them to focus on activities with greater added value for faculty and students alike and enables the so-called phenomenon of "flipping the classroom".

Flexible, adaptable, intensive, user-friendly and, yes, even entertaining: these are the hallmarks of blended learning, which combines online learning with a classroom-based approach. The advantage of high-quality and engaging online methodologies is that they keep the learning momentum going by adapting to the specific circumstances of the learner. It also allows for greater interactivity between participants.

Blended teaching methods, both in university education and in corporate learning, are here to stay and will only continue to expand. That said, there are still some analysts who downplay the importance of the impact of online learning, and those who argue that nothing can replace face-to-face teaching. (For example, P. Hunter, "Why MOOCs and executives don't mix", *Management Issues*, 28 April 2015 http://www.management-issues.com/opinion/7051/why-moocs-and-executives-dont-mix/)

At this point, it is important to highlight that I am talking here about blended programmes of the highest quality, with online modules delivered by the same academics as those giving classroom sessions to small groups of highly motivated students.

There is a tendency to assume that online teaching automatically means the cheaper option of open entry and open access as well as MOOCs (mass open online course.) This assumption is wrong. There are high-quality online and face-to-face forms of education, which fit the standards of excellence demanded from premium educational institutions. Associating technology-based learning methods with low-quality, cheapness and the massively distributed is an old fashioned and outdated cliché.

It is also widely believed that senior management is averse to online in-company training. This has been largely true until recently; we need to ask ourselves whether this is a generational problem and if the upcoming generation of CEOs, who will be quite familiar with the online environment and communication via mobile platforms, will be more receptive to these methodologies.

We need only to think back to the panelled boardrooms of a century ago with their ornate furniture, coal fires and other luxuries and compare them with their 21st century descendants who rely on digital platforms, video conferencing and other technologies to communicate globally round the clock.

Despite research showing that online learning can be at least as effective as classroom sessions – and even more transformational – there is still a widespread bias against it among educators, HR managers and executives. Interestingly enough, some 80% of teachers with no experience in online teaching say it is less effective than face-to-face teaching while the majority of educators with online experience say the results are as good if not better. Not to mention that many academics believe that online teaching will ultimately lead to layoffs. (See L Redpath, "Confronting the Bias Against On-Line Learning in Management Education", Academy of Management Learning & Education, 2012, Vol 11, No. 1, pp. 125-140.)

This bias against online teaching likewise extends to many professionals, particularly senior managers who have been educated along traditional lines and tend to associate quality education with face-to-face teaching. But what really determines the quality of a programme is its methods of teaching and learning rather than the means by which they are delivered.

Whatever the arguments, the simple truth is that those educational institutions that offer blended courses (combining quality online training with traditional classroom teaching) are growing,

and rapidly. It is very likely that in few years' time most business schools will run a majority of programmes on blended formats.

For example, the *2015 Grade Level: Tracking Online Education in the United States* survey shows that 70.8% of chief academic leaders believe online education is a critical component of their long-term strategies (up from the 48.8% who believed this back in 2002.

At the same time, 77% believe that online training produces the same or better results than traditional face-to-face teaching. Just 28% admit that their teaching staff accept the value and legitimacy of online teaching. (I E Allen and J Seaman, Grade Level: Tracking Online Education in the United States, February 2015, http://www.onlinelearningsurvey.com/reports/gradelevel.pdf.)

Another survey of corporate learning (Roland Berger, Corporate Learning Goes Digital: How companies can benefit from online education, May 2014 https://www.rolandberger.com/media/pdf/Roland_Berger_TAB_Corporate_Learning_E_20140602.pdf) estimates that in 2014 77% of US companies used e-learning for their professional development programmes while in Europe, more than 3,000 companies used these types of teaching methods. The same survey estimates that 90% of companies will be using e-learning platforms by 2017.

It is clear, then, that blended learning will play a growing role in executive education, particularly in cases where participants are unable to attend classroom sessions. The question is thus not whether blended learning is the future or whether classroom teaching is more effective than online teaching but rather: what is the optimal blend of online and face-to-face?

Obviously, achieving the right combination of online and classroom teaching depends on a programme's objectives, participant profile, content, the abilities and skills being developed, as well as costs, infrastructure, and the ability of instructors and faculty to teach online.

What are the main challenges for blended education in the near future? I believe they are mainly three:

• First, and most importantly, the adequate preparation and involvement of faculty. In

70.8%

The *2015 Grade Level: Tracking Online Education in the United States* survey shows that 70.8% of chief academic leaders believe online education is a critical component of their long-term strategies (up from the 48.8% who believed this back in 2002)

90%

A survey of corporate learning estimates that in 2014 77% of US companies used e-learning for their professional development programmes while in Europe, more than 3,000 companies used these types of teaching methods. The same survey estimates that 90% of companies will be using e-learning platforms by 2017

"
"

The question is not whether blended learning is the future or whether classroom teaching is more effective than online teaching but rather: what is the optimal blend of online and face-to-face?

the new blended environment, the professor becomes the orchestrator of the learning process, calibrating the use of different methodologies adapted to each individual participant and balancing group and personal learning. In order to achieve this, it is essential to invest in faculty development and expose them to the full educational potential of learning technologies. The basic requirement for success in this new environment is that the faculty remains forever passionate about teaching.

• Second is striking the right balance between the three different components of blended learning: face-to-face modules, which remain essential for the socialisation and integration of the class; live videoconferences and synchronous sessions (there are some developments that radically improve the look and feel of live streaming, like the "WOW Room," recently launched by IE Business School); and friendly and engaging asynchronous sessions via forums, chats, tutored-led interaction, and peer learning and feedback support.

• Third, the development of teaching materials that better adapt to this new learning context. For example, multimedia case studies set in real time, interactive group and individual simulations, personalised content and individualised assessment tools to maximise personal progress. Gamification enriches the learning experience and can be applied to nearly every context and educational content as well as serving as a vehicle for instant feedback. There are even those who argue that it can help change personal behaviour and, perhaps most appealing, that it has a positive impact on the bottom line.

Technology will certainly contribute to the humanisation of learning. However, in this new and fascinating context of education, the competitive advantage of a business school will rest on the unique experience it provides to students.

Content may be prince; technology may be king; but experience is emperor.

ABOUT THE AUTHOR
Professor Santiago Iniguez de Onzono is President, IE University, Spain.

Section_04
Uncertain Futures and Transformational Change

"Undergraduate courses in business are the largest majors in both the UK and the US (and probably globally) and arguably have much more significance in the education of future managers than post-graduate programmes"

Howard Thomas
'Apply liberally – Towards a model of liberal management education'

 Audio version

Volume

Issue

14_01

2019

Apply liberally

Towards a model of liberal management education

Howard Thomas argues the case for integrating the liberal arts into management education so that the existing curricula emphasis on technological and analytical acumen is balanced with skills of critical thinking and ethical intelligence necessary for managerial judgement

My focus here is on undergraduate business programmes, even though the plea for the stronger adoption of liberal management education applies equally to postgraduate programmes in management education, including the MBA.

Undergraduate courses in business are the largest majors in both the UK and the US (and probably globally) and arguably have much more significance in the education of future managers than post-graduate programmes.

My starting point is the *Carnegie Foundation Programme Report*, written in 2011, admittedly from an US perspective, which called for a radical rethinking of undergraduate management education.

The agenda of management education has been highjacked over time, mainly in the postgraduate arena. Rakesh Khurana, an American educator at Harvard University and Harvard Business School, for example, notes that there is no longer a consensus on what constitutes a core curriculum in business. Skills of analysis (the model of logical positivism) have been prioritised. This has been at the expense of skills necessary for managerial judgement and the process of managing organisational environments of increasing challenge, complexity and ambiguity.

Indeed, there are a series of consistent weaknesses in the development of a range of managerial capabilities from creative, critical thinking to integrative problem framing and solving that would enhance both business and analytic skills.

So what is liberal management education?

What we call liberal management education in our new book (Stefano Harney and Howard Thomas, *The Liberal Arts and Management Education: A Global Agenda for Change*, Cambridge University Press, December 2019) would ground the study of the business world in an understanding of the wider world.

Rather than focusing solely on technical and business skills, management education would welcome the humanities and social sciences at the foundation of its curriculum and the two forms of education, professional and liberal, would be melded and integrated into a holistic curriculum.

Above all, this curriculum would not be characterised by a narrow, functional specialisation but would give management students access to the vast literature on enlightenment thinking in the humanities and to approaches about the role of history and society in the social sciences. Management is surrounded by paradox and ambiguity and hence requires broad-based holistic thinking and the development of important skills of synthesis, criticism, and intellectual curiosity as well as insights into analytic thinking.

Indeed, the lately canonised Cardinal Newman in his 19th century book *The Idea of a University* and elsewhere proposed that professional education should not belong in any university. He believed in a moral authority and freedom of thought, provided by a liberal education, and argued that simply acquiring knowledge without simultaneously cultivating liberal intellectual skills would result in a poor, inadequate education.

In his view, the purpose of a liberal education is to develop those critically important skills of analysis, criticism and synthesis and to use them to leverage knowledge acquisition wisely and effectively.

Thus, the goal in management education should be to provoke the development in the student of what we would call "criticality", creativity and analytical ability as well as an ethical, social and cultural ordering of the world.

In this manner, management students would then be prepared as leaders of society committed to both an ethical world and an ethical business environment.

Stories matter, so I will give you an example of an evolving liberal management education model from Asia, which draws upon my experiences as a Dean at Singapore Management University (2009 – 2015). As background, I arrived in SMU when the global financial crisis was still a festering wound with economic austerity as its signature policy element.

The only consolation for deans of management at that time was that while the financial crisis could partially be attributed to a massive systemic failure (with a narrative very similar to that of the great crash of 1929 – 39), the current failure in "Euroland" is clearly a failure of political will and leadership.

"

*The challenge we found in curriculum
design was that to achieve sustainable
inclusive growth in emerging markets
such as Asia, the focus must be based
on the proposition that the mission of
business and the purpose of growth
is to build a better society for everyone,
and not just a simplistic objective
of maximising shareholder wealth*

Therefore, the challenge we faced in designing an Asian management education was to evolve new forms of management education which would teach students how to avoid some of the pitfalls associated with the collapse of Lehman Brothers in 2008-09 and the ongoing euro-crisis in order to help them navigate an ethical and cultural environment vastly different from that of even a decade ago.

As we attempted to rise to this challenge, a fundamental starting point was that management education cannot be divorced from the historical and cultural context within which it is taught. In Asia, therefore, it was important to discover, develop and then teach the unique historical, philosophical and cultural contexts within which Asian civilisations achieved their success as well as identifying what might lead to their decline and fall.

Thus, a management education student would be forced to go well beyond the study of business functions to also be a student of history, politics, cross-border communication and cultural exchange.

This also implied that as Asia emerged as an important economic region, mainly via the offices of the Association of South East Asian nations (ASEAN), the curriculum needed also to examine the reasons for the rise of the West, such as the role of science and the focus on the empirical method of proof. It is no accident that in contemporary Asia, every child is told to focus on science.

However, an Asian curriculum should not simply adopt US or European models of capitalism as its underlying rationale and identity. The recurring socio-ethical traditions of south-east Asia (rather like the *ubuntu* tradition and spirit in Africa) are of a communitarian, family-focused web of mutual obligations. This communitarian characteristic challenges both the rule of law and the highly individualistic, Darwinian ethos of US capitalism or the state-welfare tendencies of Euro-capitalism.

Communitarian capitalism can therefore be characterised as more stakeholder and less shareholder driven. Thus, the interests of the community of stake holders in an enterprise – the owners, employees, larger communities – would be a higher consideration than simply return on capital in a western context. These ideas have until recently have been somewhat heretical in the design of business school curricula in the West.

Hence, to really understand this communitarian ethos, which has certainly underpinned the east Asian cultural heritage, required our Asian students in management education to undergo a foundational, general educational curriculum in the fundamental philosophical, social, historical and literary traditions of Asian civilisations.

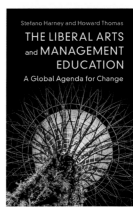

Stefano Harney and Howard Thomas

THE LIBERAL ARTS
and MANAGEMENT
EDUCATION
A Global Agenda for Change

The structure of this undergraduate programme has evolved and become much more Asian in orientation over the last two decades. From its inception the undergraduate programme has been a path-breaker in undergraduate education in Singapore. Some of the highlights included small class size, interactive teaching involving project-based learning, a community service project, global exposure, study abroad and international components as well as the common curriculum, which comprises 40% of the programme.

The initial common core of the curriculum incorporated basic foundation courses such as maths and academic writing, a university core emphasising many of the skills advocated by Newman and others, a broad-based general education requirement, global and regional studies, and the importance of technology and global awareness.

In its more recent evolution, the curriculum has focused even more closely on learning outcomes and required graduate characteristics including the following: awareness of disciplinary and multi-disciplinary knowledge; developing both intellectual and creative skills; addressing interpersonal skills; promoting global citizenship; and, finally, developing personal mastery in terms of trust, integrity and independence in decision making.

Finally, SMU's core curriculum has continually evolved and now has a focus on Singapore and Asian studies embracing three pillars: Capabilities, Communities and Civilisation. This core now amounts to about a third of the programme, with further elective flexibility and the opportunity to graduate with single or double majors in the field of management. An internship, a community service project, as well as a study abroad experience are also mandated in the programme.

Hence, evolution of the core curriculum demonstrates SMU's clear commitment to broad-based, multi-disciplinary learning, critical thinking and communication skills while training students about the profession of management.

For example, in Asia, the role of government-controlled enterprises such as sovereign wealth funds and government itself as well as the strong influence of family-controlled companies are arguably greater than in the West. Therefore, in addressing the linguistic and cultural differences in Asia we designed our Asian curriculum to require a much deeper understanding of Asian traditions and social trends.

The challenge we found in curriculum design was that to achieve sustainable inclusive growth in emerging markets such as Asia, the focus must be based on the proposition that the mission of business and the purpose of growth is to build a better society for everyone, and not just a simplistic objective of maximising shareholder wealth.

So, finally, let us explain how a liberal management education model has evolved in the context of SMU. SMU admitted its first set of students in 2000 and was set up as the third national university in Singapore but with a four-year undergraduate degree unlike the three-year model favoured by the National University of Singapore (NUS) and Nanyang Technological University (NTU).

About the Author

Howard Thomas is Emeritus Professor of Strategic Management and Management Education at Singapore Management University, Singapore, and Ahmass Fakahamy Professor Global Leadership at the Questrom School of Business, Boston University, US

Section_04
Uncertain Futures and Transformational Change

"Leading business schools have become important paradigms of excellence. Many have globalised education in ways much older and renowned universities have never done"

Jordi Canals
'Can they fix it?'

 Audio version

Volume   Issue

04_01

gf

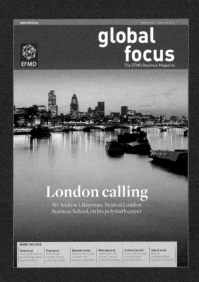

2010

Jordi Canals looks at the main drivers of business schools' success in the 20th century along with some of the major problems and challenges they will have to deal with in the future if they want to remain relevant

Can they fix it?

" "

The many leadership and managerial challenges of the 21st century will sustain strong demand for professional managers and entrepreneurs

Business schools are young institutions. They first appeared about a century ago in America, 50 years or so ago in Europe and much less than that in other parts of the world.

But, generally, in that short time they have had a positive impact on people, companies and society. There is wide experience of the positive effects of their programmes in the lives of many people and the success of many companies.

Some failures and mistakes (including those related to the 2007 financial crisis) cannot hide the basic fact that the effects of business schools in developing professionals and through them fostering job creation, investment, innovation and new firms has been impressive.

In addition, leading business schools have become important paradigms of excellence. Many have globalised education in ways much older and renowned universities have never done.

The many leadership and managerial challenges of the 21st century will sustain strong demand for professional managers and entrepreneurs. Business schools will continue to have a decisive role in educating them and providing society with the managerial talent needed to face these challenges.

While it is true that business schools prospered in the benign economic conditions of the second half of the last century it is also true that their impact on entrepreneurs and professional managers was at least partially responsible for that economic growth in the first place.

Though individual business schools took different approaches, all, both in America and Europe, adopted a similar model that was the key to their success.

This model was based on an academically qualified full-time faculty that carried out relevant research and attracted a high-quality student body. These in turn proved highly

effective recruits inside companies, increasing corporate interest in using business schools as recruiting and training grounds.

The positive experience of both alumni and companies was key in funding business school endowment, particularly in America – an effect that was vitally important to building financially solid educational institutions.

This model has been the linchpin of the success of business schools. Nevertheless, it has created its own problems. Moreover, the business context in which graduates have to work has also changed significantly.

The current financial crisis and the eroding of corporate reputations have given rise to strong criticisms of business schools and their role in those events. For these reasons, business schools will have to change if they want to keep having a positive impact on people, firms and societies.

These criticisms fall into two categories. The first is related to factors external to business schools, mainly the financial crisis, globalisation, and the notion of the firm and its reputation. The second category has to do with internal deficiencies or deficits in business schools themselves.

External factors
The role of business schools in the crisis
As happened with the dotcom crisis at the end of the 20th century, many are pointing fingers at business schools over the current financial crisis.

Though many MBA graduates did indeed end up in financial institutions, their relative overall numbers were not large. The claim that business schools were the main "feeders" of investment banks is not accurate.

A more important question is whether schools could have provided better frameworks of business and ethics and, more important, better ways of integrating ethics with finance and strategy; or whether senior managers educated in good graduate schools could have done more to avoid disaster. And, more importantly, whether those graduates could have provided a better example of professionalism and integrity.

Globalisation

Together with the current economic crisis, globalisation and its impact on the business world is another area of concern. Many Western companies have failed in their efforts to become more efficient in their international operations.

In this area, business schools have not done a good job in making clear and explicit the specific demands of globalisation, cross-cultural management and the variety of dimensions, experiences, and human and cultural values to be taken into account.

The crisis and corporate reputation

The third relevant factor is the serious damage to corporate reputations that has unfolded over the past decade. In many countries, companies used to be admired institutions that created jobs, generated investment and were drivers of progress.

Public opinion in some countries now sees business leaders as opportunists with a short-term focus on their own benefits and privileges and responsible for many of today's corporate disasters.

Business schools have been slow in reacting to these challenges. As institutions educating managers and business leaders, business schools have to rethink the role of companies in society, the job of business leaders and how to include these dimensions in their programmes.

Internal factors

Unfortunately, the challenges for business schools do not come only from the outside world. Their own development and success have sown the seeds of serious internal challenges that must be tackled.

There are some areas with major deficits at many business schools: mission, governance, humanistic approach, financial and relevance.

Mission deficit

Some business schools do not have a clear sense of mission of the role they want to play in society. It is clear that all of them want to help educate people and develop new knowledge. The question is what balance between those two activities business schools want to have.

There is no single answer but it is nevertheless important to understand why a business school exists and what it wants to do. Each school has its own views but it is good to make them explicit and connect them with its strategy, faculty development, programme design and research initiatives.

Governance deficit

Business schools are influential institutions. As such, their governance matters. Unfortunately, academic institutions in general have a poor track record in this area.

There are several levels of governance in business schools to look at.

The first is the relationship between the parent university and the business school, a link that can mostly lead to situations of lack of autonomy, both strategic and financial.

Second is the accountability and powers of the dean and senior faculty. There is no single best model here but it is certainly an issue not always well defined in business schools.

The third is the role of faculty in designing programmes, shaping research initiatives, promoting their peers to tenured positions and shaping the strategy of the school. Good governance requires a stronger faculty commitment to the long-term development of their schools.

Good governance needs to give faculty an appropriate role in business schools, one that neither blocks change nor makes faculty members alienated from the management of the school.

Humanistic deficit

In the early part of the 20th century prominent business people believed that companies had a social purpose beyond just making money.

IMAGE COURTESY OF AIESEC

||||||||||||||||||||||||||||||
❝❞
As institutions educating managers and business leaders, business schools have to rethink the role of companies in society and the job of business leaders

IMAGE COURTESY LONDON BUSINESS SCHOOL

of research similar to that of other social sciences schools. Unfortunately, this research, even if (or perhaps because) it was adorned with an allegedly superior academic rigour, became increasingly irrelevant to management practice.

A relevance deficit also became clear in schools' programmes. Many top US business schools did not offer executive programmes until quite recently. It was, in part, a matter of choice but also attributable to the lack of faculty interest in working with senior executives on real business problems.

However, the risk of irrelevance in research is smaller when faculty members have to work in a classroom with senior executives. Working with experienced managers stretches the capabilities and expertise of faculty and makes them more aware of real corporate problems.

Financial deficit

American business schools used to rely on their endowments to pay higher salaries or attract students and were consequently less dependent on academic fees. In Europe schools had to be closer to the real world with more emphasis on executive education.

In both cases, there is a problem. For American schools the endowment model is good when stock prices go up but becomes a nightmare when market prices fall. For European business schools, executive education is a distinguished undertaking for many reasons but in some cases business schools only do it for financial reasons, which is not the best motivator.

The challenge for business schools is to develop an economic model that can make them sustainable in the long term. There is no single formula. Each school has to design its own pattern. Their development will be one more test of how well a business school is run.

New challenges for business schools

There are some other ingredients in the current model of business schools that require additional work. Companies, recruiters and executives expect this. Some have been referred to earlier. Below are highlighted others that have been neglected and are more difficult to tackle: integration, leadership development, a humanistic view of the firm, life-long learning and organisational structure.

||||||||||||||||||||||||||||||||||

"

The challenge for business schools is to develop an economic model that can make them sustainable in the long term

The creation of business schools through the generosity of major donors was related to the conviction that the education of general managers in a rigorous and ethical way was important for the good of society.

Management and financial theories and the stronger role of capital markets as drivers of modern capitalism have displaced some of those early ideals. Getting results, irrespective of what happens to individuals working in the organisation, has become the dominant paradigm in the practice of management.

The outcome has been the growth of more impersonal organisations where individuals are just one more resource and a rise in employee dissatisfaction. The claim that people are important is stronger than ever; but, in practice, many decisions are taken without considering their impact on people.

Business schools have contributed to the spread of this view by underplaying the role of individuals in organisations and business decisions.

Relevance deficit

After the second world war business schools became relevant institutions because they helped tackle a very important need: the education of professional managers and the development of a body of knowledge about the main management disciplines.

In the 1970s and 1980s many business schools became more interested in promoting a type

Integration

The modern firm as it developed was built around business functions: purchasing, manufacturing, logistics, marketing, sales and so on. Over the past few decades, many companies have grown in complexity. Some basic processes can still be managed and run on a functional basis but many others require a more complex organisational design.

Unfortunately, business schools in general have not been very quick to react. Business programmes and research are still based around business functions. This is not wrong. What is wrong is what happens with courses where the reflection, diagnosis and decisions around business problems are considered exclusively from the perspective of the specific business functions (marketing, finance, operations, and so on) not the perspective of the whole company.

Teaching integrated courses is an important step. But helping people think in an integrated way is a transformational experience business schools should aim at.

Leadership development

An indirect effect of the lack of integration in business education is the fact that there are not many coherent and comprehensive models of leadership development or management.

As with integration and cross-disciplinary, cross-functional learning, leadership development is a complex process. And it is one that many schools leave to the spontaneity of students and faculty.

Moreover, many schools have neither a view of what a senior manager is and what he or she should do nor how to educate for those capabilities if they did know.

Humanistic view of the firm

The dominant economic and sociological paradigms in management have produced a simplified and warped view of the individual in organisations. It replaces the notion of individual freedom with determinism. Given the right incentives or the right environment, people will always behave in a certain way. And the role of incentives and the environment is to shape human behaviour at the service of organisations' goal of maximising profits.

This assumption is at odds with one of the basic tenets of many companies and management scholars who highlight the importance of these humanistic roots:

people do matter. There is a need to make firms more human, moving beyond the notion of pure efficiency.

Life-long learning

The explosion of diversity and complexity in all areas of knowledge makes a significant part of the educational process obsolete more quickly than in the past. This is obvious in scientific disciplines such as physics, biology or chemistry. And it is becoming evident in business leadership and management. This requires a commitment to life-long learning and education.

Continuous education and learning is obviously a big challenge. But it also is a great opportunity for business schools. Many graduates are eager to keep learning, develop new capabilities or think about a second or a third professional life. In addition, companies and society need business schools to keep contributing to the development of managers' knowledge and capabilities.

This challenge requires that schools adopt a new strategy, more open to considering undergraduate and graduate programmes as initial steps in a professional development process. They also need to think about executive education programmes not as a portfolio of disparate areas and topics but as a way that may help cover the new educational needs of individuals and companies.

Conclusion

This article has briefly examined some complex and demanding needs that have an impact on business schools and how their mission is perceived by the business world and society. Business schools alone cannot solve these problems.

Nevertheless, business schools and their faculties have the potential to help address many of them. Even if the challenges are huge, the need for excellent business schools is even deeper today than it was a century ago when the first schools were founded. The opportunities for great educational programmes and relevant research are bigger than ever. **gf**

||||||||||||||||||||||||||||||||||

" "

Even if the challenges are huge, the need for excellent business schools is even deeper today than it was a century ago when the first schools were founded

FURTHER INFORMATION
This article is an edited version of a longer article *Business schools in the twenty-first century: Strategic, organizational and managerial challenges*, a chapter to be published in the book *The future of leadership development: The role of business schools* in 2010.

ABOUT THE AUTHOR
Jordi Canals is Dean of IESE business school

gf

Section_04
Uncertain Futures and Transformational Change

"To defeat the shadows, business schools should become light bearers of hope, change, and global community"

Johan Roos
'Casting Light in the Shadows'

 Audio version

Volume   Issue

11_01

2016

Do not be lulled by today's strong management education market, says **Johan Roos**. Business schools still need to find a grander vision of hope, change and community to counter emerging shadows

Casting light in the shadows

Business school deans are smiling and optimistic these days. Things have improved since the 2008 crisis. Applications are skyrocketing at most schools, enrolments are up and, with a few notable exceptions, the crucial role of business in economic affairs and global progress is recognised and respected. We can boast that there are over 10,000 business schools around the globe and about one-fifth of the world's students are studying business and management.

What is especially laudatory about this situation is the burgeoning interest in entrepreneurialism, as millennials and older students are eager to start innovative new companies. The possibilities to develop new products, services and solutions are unprecedented in human history.

Even more encouraging for the future of humanity is that some of this entrepreneurialism is devoted to global transformation. Dubbed social entrepreneurship, we see students and their faculty advisors in business schools throughout the world innovating new solutions to help erase poverty, teach skills to the uneducated, empower women, expand and improve healthcare, and more.

Anti-progress forces cast a growing shadow

Despite the good news, I am writing to warn that there is a shadow hanging over this seemingly rosy outlook. In his October 2016 essay in *The Economist*, President Obama captured the paradox we face today: "The world is more prosperous than ever before and yet our societies are marked by uncertainty and unease".

Business schools and their deans cannot disregard this darkness that threatens to halt the progress most of the world has made since 2008 to rebuild capitalism and strengthen social democracies. I am not referring to the threat of external terrorism from *jihadis* but rather to internal forces within most Western nations that are the consequences of our own neglect in dealing forthrightly with lingering economic and social problems.

The consequences are unparalleled as strong "anti-progress" forces that encompass a variety of evolutionary or revolutionary movements coalesce power. These collectively function to

1/5

There are over 10,000 business schools around the globe and about one-fifth of the world's students are studying business and management protest, prevent and even sabotage policies and practices that most agree are beneficial to humanity. I see five elements that comprise this shadow: the rise of the "precariat", anti-globalism, anti-intellectualism, extreme inequality and tolerance of greater asymmetry.

The rise of the precariat

Precariat is the term used by economist Guy Standing in his books *The Precariat – The New Dangerous Class* (Bloomsbury 2011) and *The Corruption of Capitalism* (Biteback 2016) to describe a new social class who face overlapping challenges of unemployment, low income and loss of social security. It includes tens of millions of blue-collar workers but also frustrated educated youths who do not get the jobs and income they expected even if they have a university degree, as well as oppressed women and migrants without much hope.

For people of the precariat, a life of work remains unfulfilled because, for the first time in history, wages have not risen with increased productivity, corporate profits and employment levels. Advances such as artificial intelligence, which have enabled automation that may replace more than a few job categories over the next few years, add to the insecurity, instability and vulnerability of the precariat experience. According to Standing, the precariat are and will continue to be incomparably worse off than workers with stable, fixed-hour jobs, paid vacation and other social benefits.

This tribe is as much anti-state as it is anti-business. They believe that the rules for distribution of income and social goods are rigged against them. They are angry and find comfort in autocratic political leaders who profess anti-global, anti-trade, anti-intellectual notions and who blame minorities, immigrants and the "establishment" for our social ills. We all should take heed of Standing's most recent message: the precariat's vulnerability today is everyone's tomorrow.

Precariat is the term used to describe a new social class who face overlapping challenges of unemployment, low income and loss of social security. It includes tens of millions of blue-collar workers but also frustrated educated youth who do not get the jobs and income they expected even if they have a university degree, as well as oppressed women and migrants without much hope

Anti-globalism

For centuries, international trade has helped advance the free world and is an economic orthodoxy among most economists today. Nobody denies that globalisation has flaws; an open economy creates winners and losers. Debating the merits of global trade and globalisation itself can be valuable but few doubt that international trade is a necessity in a modern business world. However, peddlers of protectionism and nativism argue that globalism is good for the elite only.

Protests against major trade agreements across the Atlantic and Pacific demonstrate how contentious free trade ideas are among people who associate globalisation with lost industrial glory, lost full-time jobs and weakened social identity. The 2016 backlash leading up to the Brexit referendum in the UK and the similar reaction evident in the recent US presidential election campaign, which launched Donald Trump into the White House, illustrate the discrepancy between the well-articulated logic by people on top of the pyramid compared to the realities felt by the squeezed and angry precariat.

Anti-intellectualism appears not only in the US but in other Western and emerging nations where science is doubted and questioned; where art, literature and music are disrespected; and where propaganda and disinformation overtake true freedom of thought

99%

Anti-intellectualism also occurs even among the educated; in the US, 99% of scientists accept evolution as a fact...

50%~

....while almost half of college graduates believe it is just a theory

Anti-intellectualism

Anti-intellectualism appears not only in the US but in other Western and emerging nations where science is doubted and questioned; where art, literature and music are disrespected; and where propaganda and disinformation overtake true freedom of thought.

This anti-intellectualism may reflect the growing ranks of high school dropouts, non-college educated youth, senior citizens on the brink of poverty and the unemployed precariat class. But it also occurs even among the educated; in the US, 99% of scientists accept evolution as a fact while *almost half of college graduates* believe it is just a theory.

Evolution-deniers, history repudiators, conspiracy theorists and state-funded internet trolls are equally culpable of spreading doubt about scientific truths and poisoning a positive view of intellectualism and enlightenment. Politicians and media figures who shamelessly produce lie after lie plant seeds of doubt about society's basic institutions and tout a wide range of unscientific, irrational explanations about everything that further fuels anti-intellectualism.

To a degree, anti-intellectualism springs from a great failure to educate youth and adults in critical thinking. School is becoming a place for skills training, losing sight of the need for a broad education that produces responsible citizens who can think deeply and expressively.

The true meaning of liberal arts education is to cultivate "free" (Latin *liber*) individuals who are prepared to constructively deal with uncertainty and ambiguity. The result should be open-minded people resistant to dogma and preconceptions and who are sceptical enough to think for themselves. This element of the shadow should be extremely disconcerting to everyone in academia.

 We must develop solutions to boost the currently hopeless precariat into participating in economic growth and wealth; we must create equitable and fair trade agreements; we must combat the ignorance of anti-intellectualism; we must truly solve the wealth inequality challenge; and we must inspire the business world to participate in balancing out the many types of asymmetry on the planet

Extreme inequality

A tolerance for income and wealth inequality is a fourth force for anti-progress and is spreading globally. China has created more billionaires than the US and India boasts a large new class of multi-millionaires. Economist after economist has warned us that the business world has allowed the rate of return on capital to skyrocket relative to the rate of economic growth, meaning that profits and benefits of business flow to far too few people.

In his 2016 book *The Corruption of Capitalism* Standing lambasts the capitalist "elite" that is enriching itself not through production of goods and services but through ownership of assets and intellectual property aided by state subsidies, tax breaks, debt mechanisms and the privatisation of public services.

Regardless of who they are and how they gain their wealth, the repercussions on society of the current mega-inequality risk creating a domino effect that counters progress. In his recent essay in *The Economist*, President Obama warns that "a capitalism shaped by the few and unaccountable to the many is a threat to all".

Tolerance of greater asymmetry

The fifth force I see darkening the horizon is the movement away from progress that the world was clearly making following the end of the Cold War. The planet is tumbling increasingly towards an enormous imbalance, an asymmetrical future in which so much is wrong compared with things that are right.

Globalisation and automation are weakening the position of ordinary citizens and consequently, their ability to secure decent income, repay their debts and maintain their social security and general enlightenment.

Increasing terrorism, the failure of the European Community (2016 examples include Brexit and the near botching of a trade agreement with Canada), the inability of the UN to solve conflicts, dictatorships and increasingly authoritarian regimes, "hybrid warfare" to avoid attribution or retribution, apparently unstoppable global warming, the rising pollution of the planet's natural resources – all these trends do not bode well for humanity.

These conditions also provide fertile ground for social unrest, which is most politicians' worst nightmare. Anger and protests on the left and the right, from Occupy Wall Street to the anti-immigrant and protectionist rallies of autocratic politicians are one thing but violent demonstrations, marshal law and the threat of pitchfork and axe revolt, are quite another.

To boldly go where no man has gone before

At the height of the Cold War, Russian astrophysicist Nicolai Kardashev proposed a model for the future of humanity. He invented a scale to measure a civilization's advancement based on how much energy it can capture and utilise. His idea was that the more energy a civilisation can harness, the more technologically advanced it is.

Using Kardashev's scale, we are currently a Type 0 civilisation. We can extract energy only from crude raw materials. In contrast, Type I civilisations are capable of harnessing all the available energy of their planet and using it in sustainable ways, which some futurists predict will happen within a few hundred years if we have not by then destroyed our planet. Type II civilisations are able to capture the energy of their star, in our case the Sun. The Federation of Planets in *Star Trek* may illustrate such a culture, though it will remain in the realm of fantasy for most of us as what Kardashev called a Type III culture, extracting energy from billions of stars to travel across intergalactic space.

To elevate our human species to anything above a pitiful Type 0 civilization we must achieve greater cultural and intellectual sophistication, not just more advanced technology. This calls for stability, effective conflict resolution and a genuine sense of global community. If we do not arrive at that point, the downside for Planet Earth is bleak.

Towards a new vision for business schools

As deans and faculty preparing so many young people to become the next generation of business and government leaders moving towards a Type 1 civilization, we cannot shirk from trying to prevent this shadow from overtaking us. If business is to be the leading change agent to transform the world and contribute to solving humanity's most critical problems, we must subscribe to a grander vision for the role that business schools play in creating our collective future. What would this entail?

The easy answer would be to focus on the grander challenges such as countering the five shadow forces enumerated above. To some extent we do. In 2003, EFMD published a manifesto, *Initiative towards sustainable societal and business management development*, which sets out a vision for making global responsibility a major thrust in management education.

In a similar grand aspiration, the 2016 AACSB *Collective vision for business education* calls for business schools to step into the light and stop being "underdeveloped, undervalued, and too-often unnoticed".

In this vision, business schools become:
1. catalysts for innovation;
2. co-creators of knowledge;
3. hubs of lifelong learning;
4. leaders on leadership; and
5. enablers of global prosperity.
   Who could disagree?

But I suggest we need to go further. We must develop solutions to boost the currently hopeless precariat into participating in economic growth and wealth; we must create equitable and fair trade agreements and combat the myopic anti-trade and anti-globalisation forces; we must combat the ignorance of anti-intellectualism, which has reactionary beliefs at its core; we must truly solve the wealth inequality challenge that is worsening year by year in many countries; and we must inspire the business world to participate in balancing out the many types of asymmetry on the planet. Combined, these actions call for a collective aspiration for business schools that extends beyond the vision we have today.

To defeat the shadow, business schools should become light bearers of hope, change, and global community. They can do this by becoming:
- not only academic researchers publishing for our peers but creators of relevant innovative solutions of benefit to the broader society
- not only catalysts of innovation but furthering the upside and help mitigating the downside of globalisation
- not only promoters of global responsibility but servants of a better society at large
- not only co-creators of knowledge but centres of liberal ideas and critical thinking
- not only hubs of lifelong learning but champions of economic equality
- not only trainers of leaders with business impact but leaders who are masters of collaboration
- not only enablers of global prosperity but open doorways to help the precariat

Let us work together to exemplify this kind of vision in our schools.

ABOUT THE AUTHOR
Professor Johan Roos is Chief Academic Officer, Hult International Business School (including Ashridge), which he joined in January 2016. Prior to joining the multi-campus Hult, he worked in six business schools and a non-profit organisation in five countries. Most recently, he was CEO and Dean of Jönköping International Business School in Sweden.

Commentary_

Where do we go now?

We should approach the future, respond to crises of the pandemic, and technological change, in a thoughtful, well-considered and purposeful manner, not an impulsive one. This requires a more strategic and purposeful, resilient approach. The cause and the goal of this resilient effort is to develop a more holistic and balanced model of management education with a higher purpose of nurturing social responsibility alongside efficiency and effectiveness and enhancing the moral and ethical compass of graduates in an increasingly uncertain world. As we have seen, progress is already being made in designing and building models of liberal, responsible management involving meaningful collaboration and co-creation across the three sectors of the economy – business, government and society.

Yet further progress is needed, and this will entail greater efforts to research and identify approaches for re-imagining management education through open-innovation and intelligence-gathering. One such effort has been the work of an open innovation research team at the Questrom School of Business at Boston University (see the Questrom website, bu.edu/jam) as well as the book *Reimagining Business Education* (Carlile *et al*, 2016).

Recent noteworthy efforts in the field include Peter Lorange's book on the Business School of the Future in which he advances his network-based strategy with entirely new roles for the faculty and campus, and also the survey-driven work on the future of business schools (Carrington Crisp) which has recently been published as a 2020 special issue, (see 'The Future: 2020', *Global Focus*).

In conclusion, it is important to recognise that dramatic changes such as the growth of digitisation, data science, AI, and other critical technologies, as well as the current pandemic crisis, require a radical rethinking of current management education paradigms. As we look to an uncertain and

> *It is important to recognise that dramatic changes such as the growth of digitisation, data science, AI, and other critical technologies, as well as the current pandemic crisis, require a radical rethinking of current management education paradigms*

ambiguous future, we will need to consider totally new ways of examining and shaping the economic and industrial environment and addressing our past 'wilful blindness' by moving from the rather harsh 'command and control' leadership involved in corporate objectives of targets and shareholder wealth maximisation to more 'humane', and human, socially responsible leadership models directed to stakeholder wealth maximization. We also have to acknowledge changes in part-time studies; successful one year pre-experience masters programmes in management; (particularly in European schools), and pedagogical changes associated with blended learning, more participative learning and project-based experiential learning; and, very importantly, our students' 'willingness to pay' increasingly expensive fees for postgraduate and executive education.

Della Bradshaw also reminds us, in examining how business schools have evolved over the last decade, of the increasing diversity of business schools' academic programmes. Her clever creation of a valuable cohort of separate but related FT rankings such as online MBAs, global MBAs, European Business Schools, Executive MBAs, Masters in Management, both post-experience And pre-experience, Masters in Finance and Executive Education (custom and open enrolment) demonstrates increasing programme specialisation

What we continue to teach in the business schools is a little like being a mapmaker in an earthquake zone. Never before has the gap between our tools and the reality of emerging industry been larger"

Gary Hamel, 1996

and competition. She also expects "this diversity to continue, with an increasing emphasis on part-time and online programmes, largely because she believes that fewer and fewer students will be prepared to take on full-time study." Technology-enabled, and blended, learning programmes will be increasingly available to ease part-time study and create flexible programmes with modular structures – so called 'stackable degrees' – to flourish in this increasingly innovative, digitally-driven marketplace.

It is also worth remembering the criticisms of management education expressed by two very well-known practical strategists, Gary Hamel and the late C. K. Prahalad. They both believe that management educators have allowed themselves to become trapped in obsolete textbooks and case study stories of past corporate experiences. They argue very strongly that new management theories, business models and paradigms are urgently needed in today's VUCA world.

One of Hamel's quotes (by now already 20 years old) is particularly apt in the current context: "What we continue to teach in the business schools is a little like being a mapmaker in an earthquake zone. Never before has the gap between our tools and the reality of emerging industry been larger" (Hamel, 1996, p.113). It is possible that a mixture of complacency about past success, a historical inertia, and aversity to change in a very financially

rewarding business school environment may constrain deans from innovation and model change. Yet the pandemic has brought technology-enhanced methods, and online learning into the forefront of debates about how to design business models and frame business school futures to align with the range of challenges associated with more inclusive forms of capitalism and environmental influences such as climate change. Our children's generation want change, and want us to respond to pandemics and climate change, and also address technology awareness, social responsibility, sustainability and inequality in society. We must change.

References
Carlile, P.R., Davidson, S.H., Freeman, K.W., Thomas, H. and Venkatraman, N. (2016) *Reimagining Business Education: Insights and Actions from the Business Education Jam*. Bingley, U.K.: Emerald Publishing.
Carrington Crisp (2020) *'The Future 2020' Report*. Special Issue, Global Focus.
Lorange, P (2019) *The Business School of the Future*. Cambridge, U.K.: Cambridge University Press.
Thomas, H. and Hedrick-Wong, Y. (2019) *Inclusive Growth: The Global Challenges of Social Inequality and Financial Inclusion*. Bingley, U.K.: Emerald Publishing.